The
Lazy Girl's
Guide to Green Living

Anita Naik

PIATKUS

Visit the Piatkus website!

Piatkus publishes a wide range of best-selling fiction and non-fiction, including books on health, mind, body & spirit, sex, self-help, cookery, biography and the paranormal.

If you want to:
- read descriptions of our popular titles
- buy our books over the Internet
- take advantage of our special offers
- enter our monthly competition
- learn more about your favourite Piatkus authors

VISIT OUR WEBSITE AT: www.piatkus.co.uk

Copyright © 2007 by Anita Naik
www.anitanaik.co.uk

First published in 2007 by
Piatkus Books Limited
5 Windmill Street
London W1T 2JA

e-mail: info@piatkus.co.uk

The moral right of the author has been asserted

A catalogue record for this book is available from the British Library

ISBN 978 0 7499 2826 1

Text design by skeisch and Paul Saunders
Edited by Jan Cutler
Cover and inside illustrations by Nicola Cramp

Mixed Sources
Product group from well-managed
forests and recycled wood or fiber
www.fsc.org Cert no. TT-COC-002231
© 1996 Forest Stewardship Council

This book has been printed on paper manufactured with respect for the environment using wood from managed sustainable resources

Printed and bound in Great Britain by William Clowes Ltd, Beccles, Suffolk

For Bella and Joe

contents

acknowledgements

Special thanks to all the lazy girls who told me why they couldn't possibly go green. I hope this book helps change your minds.

introduction

Are you a self-confessed eco-worrier? Do you stress about climate change, melting ice caps and global warming? Do you promise yourself you'll recycle more often, switch off the lights as you exit rooms, walk instead of drive, and buy organic? How often do you keep your green resolutions? Once a week when the recycling van arrives or less often than your birthday?

If that rings a familiar bell it's likely you're the quintessential lazy green girl – green in your heart but not in your head; meaning, the idea of recycling, saving energy and buying organic to save the world seems like an excellent idea in theory, but you can't find the time or inclination to do it in practice. After all, let's face it, who can be bothered to take the bus to work or a trip to the recycling bin when it's raining and cold outside, or wash the mud off organic, locally grown vegetables when you can buy perfectly clean ones nicely packaged in the supermarket? And really what's the point of worrying about global warming and your part in it when the big industries of the world are busy chugging out emissions and ruining the planet second by second?

If you feel this way, you're not alone. Studies show that 80 per cent of us are seriously concerned about environmental problems such as global warming, saving energy and the rainforests, but rarely do anything more than the odd bit of recycling and/or switching off lights as we exit rooms, simply because we imagine that being green takes too much time and effort. Or maybe if you're being 100 per cent honest, you're someone who thinks (but would never ever tell anyone) that you don't have to make an effort to be green, because out there right now some hippy chick is composting all her waste and living in a tree and so doing it all for you. Or perhaps you think you don't impact that hugely on the environment and climate change seeing as it's not you cutting down the rainforest, wasting water and taking a private jet to work every day.

Whatever your take on why you're not being green, don't be fooled: all of us impact upon the environment in some way, even if you are someone who leads a small and relatively quiet life. For example, if you drive everywhere and regularly knock up a pile of household waste larger than your body, and/or even keep the tap running when you clean your teeth, or drop small bits of litter as you take a walk, you're making an impact on the environment and could easily change your ways.

The good news is that you don't have to stop shaving your armpits, become a vegetarian and take on the mantel of an eco-warrior to be green. To make a difference and do your bit for the environment there are a variety of simple, practical and easy things you can do, and they're not expensive (in fact in most cases they can save you money), they don't take huge amounts of time and, above all, they are easier than you think to implement. For example, getting serious about energy efficiency in the home and doing things such as taking your computer and TV off standby and sleep mode would make you instant savings overnight. Recycling plastics, paper, food and glass means that landfill waste sites would be reduced by half, and if we all shared car journeys (the average car has only 1.2 passengers per journey) we could reduce pollution by 60 per cent! It's all about thinking about your actions and not working on autopilot all the time.

Why should you even bother? you may be asking. Well, whatever the cynics may say, small changes have a large impact, and whereas you may not be able to stop global warming single-handedly, doing your bit and influencing others to do theirs causes a ripple effect that can lead to a large wave of change. What's more, being green will make you feel good about yourself, whether it's buying fair-trade clothes that help make someone else's life easier, riding a bike instead of driving a car and so reducing pollution, or even separating your rubbish so that it doesn't all end up in a landfill site and pollute the air for your future children's children!

Also by becoming greener in one area of your life you

may find yourself challenging your choices in other areas. For example, by thinking about what you throw away, you could find yourself questioning your role as a consumer and thinking about how much you're buying and why you're buying it. By making your home energy efficient you may find yourself wondering how much you've been wasting up until now and how you could save even more money. Even shopping differently – that is, buying local organic produce or growing your own vegetables in a window box – may also make you consider whether supermarket shopping really is cheaper or if you've just been pulled along on a marketing wave.

Whereas being green does sound expensive (and some of it is), on the whole, being an eco-girl can, and does, save you money. For starters, I hope, you'll be persuaded into consuming less, which means you'll automatically be saving money. Next, shopping for food at farmers' markets or buying local seasonal produce means less cash disappearing from your purse. Car sharing, taking public transport and walking also save you bundles of cash, as does halving your toiletries, doing less laundry and even deciding to work from home!

And this is where *The Lazy Girl's Guide to Green Living* comes in. This is a guide to eco-friendly living that offers you choices that can and will affect the environment and your life for the better. Crammed full of options, alternatives and easy choices that you may not have considered until now, this book can show you how to do everything from making your living space greener, holidaying in an eco-friendly way and even reducing, reusing and recycling without driving yourself crazy. For how to put many of the solutions in the book to good use, check out the Resources section at the back of the book. This is your personal Internet directory to green shopping, buying and living, no matter where you are in the world. So if you're currently secretly yearning to do your global bit and save the planet – this is the book for you – read it and find out how to become the ultimate lazy girl eco-warrior!

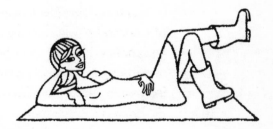

chapter 1
Green living

Do you know the size of your 'carbon footprint' (the measure of the impact your activities have on the environment)? Is it mini-me sized, or larger than a yeti? If you do everything to make your life super-easy, such as driving five minutes to the shops, buying ready-made meals, turning the washing machine on to wash just one pair of jeans and the dishwasher to clean four plates, keep all your equipment on standby and generally don't think twice about the water you use, then you have a pretty big carbon footprint that's definitely impacting upon the environment.

To establish your carbon footprint for sure, let's assume that you conform to an average lazy girl, which means that you alone are responsible for churning out 11 tonnes (10.8 tons) of carbon dioxide (CO_2) every year. If you're unsure how these add up, they could possibly include emissions from your household's gas consumption (27 per cent),

fact

The USA has the world's largest carbon footprint at 23.7 acres per person. Mozambique has the smallest at 1.3 acres, while the UK comes in at a weighty 11.6 acres per head.

and/or electricity consumption (17 per cent), possibly air travel (34 per cent), and car and public transport use (22 per cent) – and that's before you start looking at how your food and clothes impact on the environment and aid climate change.

So how's a girl to work out the size of her personal carbon footprint? Well, for starters you need to look at how much gas and electricity you use for the year – both at home and at work. Then what kind of car you've got and how far you've driven it – think small journeys and big ones. Next, think about how you get to and from work. What kind of public transport do you take, or do you walk? Then, think about how big your house is and what kind of windows and insulation you have (or don't have!). After that, think about where you go on holiday, and what gas and electricity you use when you're away, how you shop both at home and away, how you cook and eat, and finally how much you waste and throw away every day. If that calculation sounds enormous, then imagine how big your carbon footprint is right now.

fact

Generating electricity (by burning fossil fuels, such as coal) is one of the biggest producers of carbon emissions, which means that every time you make a coffee or turn the television on, dry your hair or watch a DVD you are adding to global warming.

Reducing your carbon footprint

Whereas it's impossible to eradicate your footprint totally, the good news is it is possible to go down a size or two; in fact if everyone knocked theirs back by 20 per cent the environmental impact would be huge and you could still live the life you want to live. The problem is most people believe that in order to be green they have to make huge changes and sacrifice all their luxuries, but this isn't the case. Being eco-friendly isn't about eating organic muesli, wearing hemp and walking everywhere (unless you want to, of course). It's about being conscious of your everyday actions, making the effort to do things a little differently and being more creative and eco-sensitive about your lifestyle choices.

This means you can be green and still have a car, eat the food you want, indulge your shopping habit and even have a bath, as long as you use your choices wisely. For example, if you're going to use a car, being green means using it for long journeys only, car sharing on everyday rides and also making sure your car is as green as possible (see Chapter 4 for more on this). As for having a bath, by all means have one, but just don't fill it to the brim, and make sure you recycle the water after use – that is, don't drain it all away, use it to flush your toilet or water your plants and garden (though be sure not to use bubble bath or bath oils in the water). If you're a shopping junkie go ahead and buy clothes, but recycle the clothes that you don't wear by taking them to a clothes bank or charity shop. Also, think about the labels you're wearing, where the clothes come from and how they are made (see Chapter 2 for more on this) so that you can make wiser choices about what you buy.

Simple ways with food

As for food, you don't have to buy organic to be green about what you're eating, simply buy local and you'll automatically have made an eco-friendly choice, as your food won't have clocked up thousands of food miles (the distance a product travels from field to plate).

As for the larger issues such as climate change and global warming, despite the enormity of the problem it's possible to make a difference just by making small lifestyle changes.

Whereas industry uses a huge amount of energy, our households account for 30 per cent of energy used, which means that any real change begins on our own doorsteps. So you need to think about how you use your electrical equipment, how you insulate your home and the power you use and waste, and even how you choose to clean your home. And this is what this chapter's all about: discovering how to make effective lazy girl choices that are right not only for your current lazy lifestyle but for the environment, too.

Carbon dioxide pollution

Each one of us creates CO_2 pollution through our daily lives, which then leads to global warming. Sadly, some of us have a larger impact than others – check your CO_2 score below. CO_2 pollution per person per year:

USA	20.12 tonnes (19.81 tons)
Australia	18.27 tonnes (17.98 tons)
Canada	18.20 tonnes (17.91 tons)
Russia	10.50 tonnes (10.34 tons)
Germany	9.92 tonnes (9.76 tons)
UK	9.58 tonnes (9.43 tons)
New Zealand	8.96 tonnes (8.82 tons)
South Africa	7.89 tonnes (7.77 tons)
Spain	7.47 tonnes (7.36 tons)
France	6.34 tonnes (6.24 tons)

10 reasons why you're probably not green

tip

Being green doesn't mean changing who you are, just changing what you choose to do.

So you care about the environment, you worry about global warming, animals becoming extinct, rainforests being cut down and weird genes being introduced into the food chain – so why aren't you moving your butt and doing something? Well, if you're like many lazy girls, the following probably rings true, so here's how to change your thinking and your actions.

1 It's too difficult

Being green can seem like an overwhelming thing to get to grips with, which is why it's important to think small. Forget saving the world, and ask yourself what's so difficult about throwing your bottles, cans, magazines and plastics into a green bin, instead of your usual bin, or walking by a charity shop with a bag of old clothes, or going to a bottle bank with your empties. And what's so hard about walking more, or only doing full washes in your washing machine and buying local seasonal produce instead of produce from abroad? These things may seem tiny and ineffectual but they are all green choices that have a larger impact on the world.

2 It's expensive

Being green can actually save you money because it's about thinking about what you buy and why you're buying it before you hand over the cash. Yes, some green things are more expensive, such as organic food and fair-trade produce, but not all green choices eat your money. Taking all your equipment off standby and turning down the heating saves you money in the long run (and it's more money than you think). Buying local seasonal produce at farmers' markets is cheaper than buying imported supermarket produce, and wearing what you already have before you decide to buy more saves loads of cash (after all, be honest, how many pairs of jeans and trainers does a girl need?).

3 I have no time

If you have time to eat, read a paper or magazine, buy clothes, get in your car, and have a shower, you have time to be green; as in, make green choices about what you're doing in your everyday life. For example, turn off the shower while you lather up and you'll save water; share magazines with friends and you're recycling; dispose of your food waste as compost and give a friend a lift to work, and bingo! – you're being green and good to the environment.

4 I have no idea how to do it

This is an easy one to get stuck on, so thankfully you're reading the right book, but it also pays to be pro-active, so peruse the Resources section for good ways to expand your green knowledge, contact your local council for green services in your area, and visit your local library for information on what's happening locally in the green arena.

5 It's a con

You may have read the newspaper headlines about how recycling isn't really recycled and is either dumped or shipped to other countries for money. Or how non-organic food is being sold as organic and how everything green is really one big fat con because global warming is all made up. Well, the facts are out there about global warming and while some of these recycling/organic stories are true – thanks to fraudsters who would do anything to cheat people – they are, thankfully, rare. So, don't use their bad behaviour as an excuse to sit back and do nothing.

6 What difference can one person make?

Just changing your ways can and will make a huge difference. Recycle all your waste for a week and see how much you used to just throw away without thinking. Think about what you buy for a week and see how much money you waste on products, foods and items you don't even use. Take note of all the water you go through when washing up, doing laundry, and even cleaning your teeth, and you'll see that even small everyday green changes will have a large impact on your carbon footprint.

7 I don't want to be a 'green' type

You don't have to turn into any 'type' to be green. Although the popular image of the eco-warrior is someone scruffy, vegetarian and unwashed, the reality is that eco-warriors come in all shapes and sizes, from all backgrounds and all lifestyles. Being green doesn't mean changing who you are, just changing what you do.

8 I like my luxuries

You can be green and have luxuries – check out Chapters 2, 3 and 4 on beauty, fashion, food and travel. Again, being green is not about giving up everything you like and love but about making wiser and smarter choices for the environment, your purse and the earth.

9 I'm into other issues

Being green doesn't have to overtake your life and your interests – it's simply about making fundamental changes in the way you behave in your everyday life. If you're busy campaigning for, say, AIDS or world peace, carry on, but just make sure the stuff you're doing in between is green.

10 I can't be bothered

Whereas no one can make you bothered about the environment, think about how you're going to cope in the near future when there is no oil to fuel your car, or when it's too expensive to heat up your house, or what you're going to do with your rubbish when there are no more landfill sites and it piles up on your doorstep.

How green are you?

Despite our eco-guilt, most of us, if we're honest, aren't green at home (or anywhere else for that matter) out of pure laziness. We tend to go about our daily lives on autopilot because that's the way we've always done it and/or because it's easier. If you're knowingly guilty of wasting energy because you can't be bothered to think about what you're doing, you're not only wasting a huge amount of energy but also adding to global warming, and all for no real reason apart from pure laziness, which is why step one in becoming green is to make being eco-friendly an easier choice for yourself. And let's face it, even the laziest of the lazy can do their bit, such as switching off lights as they exit rooms, turning off taps, and even recycling their glossy magazines – and just doing this can help reduce your carbon footprint and make a difference both locally and globally. So start your green quest with this short quiz to see how green your attitude is and then find out how and why you should improve it.

Quiz: *how green is your attitude?*

Tick one answer in each section and then look at the results at the end to see whether you have a green attitude.

1. When you're chilly, you …

☐ a. Whack the heating on to full blast.

☐ b. Put a jumper on.

☐ c. Have a hot bath.

2. How many items in your home are switched on right now but are not being used?

☐ a. You have no idea.

☐ b. None.

☐ c. At least four.

3. When do you recharge your mobile?

☐ a. Every night, overnight.

☐ b. When it runs out.

☐ c. For an hour every day.

4. You're moving and want to de-clutter – what do you do with the stuff you want to ditch?

☐ a. Chuck it in the bin.

☐ b. Leave it behind.

☐ c. Give it to charity.

5. Your house is smelly; what do you do?

☐ a. Open the windows.

☐ b. Use some air freshener.

☐ c. Spring-clean the house.

Results

1. A 10, B 0, C 5
Eco-friendly answer: B – the other options waste both water and energy.

2. A 10, B 0, C 5
Eco-friendly answer: B – items switched on at the mains still use energy even if they're not in use.

3. A 10, B 0, C 5
Eco-friendly answer: B – mobiles need only to be re-charged when they run out, and only for an hour.

4. A 10, B 5, C 0
Eco-friendly answer: C – a clearout is a good recycling opportunity.

5. A 0, B 10, C 5
Eco-friendly answer: A – open a window and avoid polluting your air with chemicals.

Total scores

0–10 Eco-Chick
You're saving the planet and saving money as you go – well done, you're super-green!

15–30 Semi-Green
You know what you have to do to be eco-friendly but often can't be bothered – remember: small changes have a large impact.

35–50 Energy-Waster
You use and waste an excessive amount of energy – you need to beef up your green attitude and try harder.

Easy green living

If you've scored pretty badly in the quiz above, help is at hand. Here's how to be green the lazy way:

■ **You're too lazy to go to the recycling bin**
Eco-friendly option Place a box or bag for recycling right

next to your kitchen bin. This will remind you to recycle every single time you walk to the bin.

▪ You're too lazy to remember to switch things off

Eco-friendly option Put a 'switch off' sticker next to your make-up remover, so that every night before you go to bed you'll be reminded to switch off all lights, sockets and electrical equipment. Better still, bribe your boyfriend/ flatmate – the night-time switcher-offer in your house.

▪ You're too lazy to walk, so you drive everywhere

Eco-friendly option Get your car serviced regularly so that at least it's energy efficient (see Chapter 4 for more on this). Whereas this may be more expensive, in the long run it will save you money because your car's less likely to need a large repair job. If that doesn't suit your finances then car-share on all your journeys, from shopping trips to commutes.

▪ You're too lazy to compost your food in a composting bin

Eco-friendly option Either make sure you use as much of it as you can; that is, keep leftovers to use the next day, use vegetables before they go rotten and, most of all, think before you pour anything down the drain. Oil, leftover meat and vegetable peelings should all be thrown away, not washed away. Also ask yourself: could this be cooked and frozen, or cooked and left for another day, or given to a friend or neighbour?

■ You're too lazy to shop without your car

Eco-friendly option Start Internet shopping – you get more discounts, you don't have to carry it home and often you get free delivery.

■ You're too lazy to fill the washing machine when you do a wash

Eco-friendly option Forget the laundry basket and put all your dirty clothes straight into the washing machine, this way you can wait for the drum to get full before you do a wash.

■ You're too lazy to shower

Eco-friendly option Recycle your bath water (see below for more on this), it's easier than you think. Just keep a bucket near the bath and use the water to water your garden, if that's too much effort, suggest to your nearest and dearest that you share your bath water. And while you're at it cut back on your bath toiletries – it's no good for the garden and no good for you (see Chapter 2).

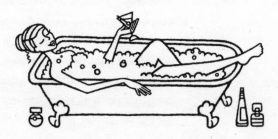

Saving energy the lazy way

Why all the fuss about saving energy, you may be thinking? Surely there are bundles of it and it's there to be used? Well, the first green issue to get your head around is that as a planet we are actually running short of the sources of energy we use every day, such as oil, gas and coal (also known as fossil fuels), with oil sources looking to be depleted in just 40 years. The latter is a massive global problem, as we all depend on oil for everything such as food, transport and industry; meaning that without it how will we drive our cars, manufacture our foods and keep our jobs?

Gas also won't last indefinitely, and although coal is abundant it causes high pollution levels, which again affect the environment. In some places coal pollution is so bad that a report by the World Health Organization noted that of the ten most polluted cities in the world, seven can be found in China, and this is all down to coal. What's more, sulphur dioxide and soot caused by coal combustion have resulted in acid rain falling on about 30 per cent of China's total land area, causing urban smog.

The second problem is that in using too much energy we're causing intense environmental damage, known as global warming.

Our part in climate change

The Intergovernmental Panel on Climate Change (around 2,000 scientists who include most of the world's best climatologists) believe that global warming is serious, and that we all need to acknowledge that human activity is playing a discernible part in it.

Surrounding the earth there is a blanket of gases which regulates the earth's climate and allows it to sustain life, but, thanks to the way we're all working our way through fossil fuels and cutting down rainforests, a large amount of gases are being released into the atmosphere, making this blanket thicker and thicker, and so causing it to act like a greenhouse (hence the term 'greenhouse gases'). This in turn has increased the earth's temperature. Whereas no one can be 100 per cent specific about the effect this temperature rise will have in the long run, it is already causing a climate change that has led to the melting of ice caps, flooding, drought and unpredictable weather such as more frequent hurricanes across the world. The main culprit is carbon dioxide and, unfortunately, burning fossil fuels releases about 6.5 billion tonnes (6.4 billion tons) of CO_2 into the atmosphere each year.

To help stop this we each have to look at our carbon footprints and work out how much we contribute towards this use of energy; meaning, how much your lifestyle impacts upon the environment. Whereas it's difficult to work out precisely how big your carbon footprint is, to be green you need to start by thinking about what you're doing at home, at work and at play every day and make small but effective changes. You may wonder what difference that will make, but the reality is that every tonne (ton) of CO_2 that you can avoid emitting into the atmosphere will help reduce the risk of global warming and climate change.

Lazy girl energy facts

- A quarter of all carbon emissions come from the fuels we use in our homes.
- Europe's fridges/freezers account for 62 million tonnes (61 million tons) of CO_2 emissions every year.
- Eight per cent of energy supplied to households is wasted on electronic equipment left on standby and equals 4 million tonnes (tons) of CO_2 annually.
- Ninety per cent of households have a washing machine that does 274 cycles a year; each cycle gets through 50–120 litres (11–26 gallons) of water.

Lazy girl energy-saving tips

You can cut your CO_2 emissions, say WWF (World Wildlife Fund), by about 9,000 kilograms (20,000 pounds) a year with very easy actions that don't take long to do and won't always cost you a fortune:

1. The next time you get a utility bill, choose a supplier who offers clean renewable energy (wind power, solar power, hydroelectric power). To see if it is available where you live, check out your country's utility companies on the Web.
   CO_2 savings per year = 3,100 kilograms (7,000 pounds).

2. If you have to drive and can't face getting a bike, consider driving a hybrid or fuel-efficient car.
   CO_2 savings per year = 2,300 kilograms (5,200 pounds).

3. Recycle. Recycling saves heaps of energy needed to make new products. Recycle 50 per cent of your glass, plastics and paper.
   CO_2 savings per year = 1,090 kilograms (2,400 pounds).

4. Turn your heating down by 3 degrees in the winter.
   CO_2 savings per year = 470 kilograms (1,050 pounds).

5. Buy a programmable thermostat; this will automatically lower your monthly energy bill by giving your heat and air conditioning a break while you are asleep or out.
   CO_2 savings per year = 470 kilograms (1,050 pounds).

6. Replace a worn-out refrigerator with an Energy Star model. The US would need 30 less power plants if all Americans used the most efficient refrigerators.
   CO_2 savings per year = 450 kilograms (1,000 pounds).

7. Turn off your computer overnight. A standard monitor left on overnight uses enough energy to print 5,300 sheets of paper.
   CO_2 savings per year = 430 kilograms (950 pounds).

8. Drive 24 kilometres (15 miles) less each week. Shrink your gas costs and your waistline by walking, biking and taking public transportation.
   CO_2 savings per year = 409 kilograms (900 pounds).

9. Avoid idling at traffic lights and in traffic. Give your engine and the climate a break by turning off your car when you aren't moving. Try to cut out ten minutes of daily idling.
   CO_2 savings per year = 250 kilograms (550 pounds).

10. Wash clothes in cold or warm water. Skip the hot water on two loads per week. You'll save energy and should have less wrinkled clothes.
    CO_2 savings per year = 250 kilograms (500 pounds).

11. Use compact fluorescent (CFL) light bulbs. It's a bright idea to replace three incandescent bulbs with CFL bulbs. These use one-quarter of the energy of normal bulbs

and typically have a life span of between 8,000 and 15,000 hours, whereas normal bulbs are usually manufactured to have a life span of 750 or 1,000 hours.

CO_2 savings per year = 136 kilograms (300 pounds).

12. Keep your tyres filled. Your ride will be smoother and you'll save up to 5 per cent on your fuel tab.

CO_2 savings per year = 125 kilograms (275 pounds).

If you're too lazy to go the whole hog, do the above to save energy. There are also plenty of other (and lazier ways) to save energy. For starters, don't fill the kettle to the brim every time you want a cup of coffee or tea – just boil one cup at a time. If 15 families did this for a year 1 tonne (0.98 tons) of CO_2 emissions would be saved. Next, plug up the draughts in your house, as 15 per cent of heat loss in the home is from your windows and under doors. Seal gaps with compression seals or simply place a blanket around the gaps.

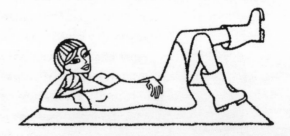

Don't be a 'standby' girl

Most importantly of all, don't be a 'standby' kind of girl. Most of us are guilty of leaving all our electrical equipment switched on for an easier life, which in turn wastes huge amounts of energy; what's more, CO_2 emissions from electrical equipment being left on are equivalent to 1.4 million long-haul flights. And it turns out your parents were right: you should always turn lights off as you leave a room – this will save you energy and money, and stop you having to replace endless light bulbs.

Saving water the lazy way

fact

In Canada the bathroom accounts for about 65 per cent of the water used and wasted inside the home, and the average American takes a shower for approximately 10.4 minutes a day!

It's an obvious fact that we all need water to survive. Just think about how much trouble it is when a mains pipe bursts and your water has to be turned off. You can't shower, make a cup of tea, wash up, cook or even get a quick drink. Despite that obvious fact, most of us don't think twice about how much water we waste every day. If you're someone who lets the tap run while you clean your teeth, has a daily bath, or stands under a hot shower for 30 minutes, puts on the washing machine to wash a couple of items or even runs the dishwasher to clean two plates, you're a water waster. Add to this all the water that gets wasted through leaking taps, flushing the toilet and watering your garden, and the amount of water you use every week is HUGE.

The reality is that in the developed world the average person gets through around 135 litres (30 gallons) every day compared to someone in the developing world, who uses around 10 litres (2 gallons)!

You may think, what's the big problem? Well, the problem is that only 1 per cent of the water supply on earth is available for human consumption and our long-term supply of clean water is running out, as we demand more and more water. This is because the water companies have to extract more from existing underground reservoirs and rivers, which are already running low. This, in turn, lowers the water level, which increases the concentration of pollutants in the water. So the next time you leave the tap running while you wander off, think about the summer water ban imposed in countries like the UK and Australia due to the lack of rainfall, the devastating droughts in Africa and Asia and the fact that already one person in five has no access to safe drinking water.

To be water-friendly, try the following easy tips:

fact

Seventy-five litres (16½ gallons) of water can be wasted every day from just one dripping tap.

Lazy girl water-saving tips

1. **Only use your washing machine when it's full** Ninety per cent of households have a washing machine, and each time you put a cycle on you get through 50–120 litres (11–26 gallons) of water. To save water, only go for full loads, and lower the heat

setting to 30°C (86°F). This will clean you clothes as well as a normal 40°C (104°F) wash and save energy and money. On top of that, when your old machine finally gives up the ghost and dies on you, invest in an energy-saving machine that allows you to run shorter cycles.

2. **Turn the tap off as you clean your teeth** Leaving it on wastes 680 litres (150 gallons) of water per month, around 8,100 litres (1,800 gallons) a year!

3. **Shower rather than bathe** Whereas a nice relaxing bath is the ultimate in unwinding, showers use less water. A standard shower uses just 35 litres (7¾ gallons) of water, compared to a bath, which uses 80 litres (17½ gallons).

4. **Don't power shower** It may be the ultimate in showering, but power showers also use about 80 litres (17½ gallons) of water. If you have one installed, buy a water-restricting showerhead.

5. **Switch off as you soap up** If you're spending time lathering up your body and hair, turn off the shower to save water being wasted down the drain.

6. **Flush less often** Obviously, flush what needs to be flushed, but you can afford to let your waterworks sit for a while, as the average house flushes 50 litres (11 gallons) of water down the toilet every day. Use a water hippo or water displacement bag

in your cistern. This is a small plastic bag, which can easily be fitted into your toilet cistern. Water is retained in the bag, helping to save water every time you flush. Better still use a water-filled bottle – although check to see that it doesn't cause an overflow in your cistern when you flush. Both of these things work by saving around 3–5 litres (5¼–8¾ pints) with every flush. If one toilet is flushed ten times a day, this would equate to a water saving of 30 litres (6½ gallons) per day, enough water for a five-minute shower! Better still, invest in a low-flush or dual-flush toilet – old toilet cisterns hold about 9 litres (15¾ pints) of water, whereas new low-flush ones hold around 6 litres (10½ pints).

7. **Collect rainwater** Obviously, if you're particularly lazy this option won't appeal to the green girl inside of you, but recycling rainwater to water your garden and household plants is a fantastic way of saving water. All you need is a water butt in your garden that collects water from the down pipe connected to your roof guttering .

8. **Get to grips with grey water** Grey water is the term used for water that's already been used in your home, so this means your bath and shower water, and water from washing up in sinks. This can be used to flush the toilet (just pour it down your toilet instead of flushing) and even water your plants and garden (although think about going green with the detergent you have used first before you happily tip it into your plants).

9. **Think before you tip** Meaning, before you empty glasses half-full of water down the sink, think about saving the water in the fridge for later, or using it to water plants.

10. **Keep drinking water in the fridge** If you regularly run the tap to make sure your drinking water is cold, simply fill up a jug at the start of each day and keep it in the fridge to avoid unnecessary wastage.

11. **Turn the temperature down** Do you really need your water to be so hot that it makes your skin tingle? Turn the thermostat down and you'll save energy and water (that is, you won't want to stand under a shower for that long if it isn't steaming hot).

fact

Americans rank high among the world's champion water guzzlers. According to the Pacific Institute for Studies in Development, Environment and Security in Oakland, California, America ranks sixth in the world behind New Zealand, Armenia, Barbados, Cuba and the United Arab Emirates for per-capita water withdrawals. Europeans use significantly less water per person for domestic purposes than do Americans. On average the Germans and French, for example, use 40 per cent less water than do Americans, roughly 250–272 litres (55–60 gallons) daily.

Reducing your waste and recycling the lazy way

The average person in Europe throws out their body size in waste and rubbish every seven weeks. If you think that no way could that be you, then try recycling everything for just one week and then check how empty your bin is and how full your recycling box is. According to the statistics, 26–30 million tonnes (25.5–29.4 tons) of rubbish is produced by households in the UK every year (that's 500 kilograms (1,102 pounds) per person per year), 14 million tonnes (13.7 tons) is produced by households in Australia per year and in America, 40 million, 80 per cent of which can be recycled if only we bothered. So why should you bother to sort your trash? Well, for starters think about where your rubbish ends up. It usually gets dumped in a landfill site (that is, buried underground) or incinerated, neither of which are ideal options for the environment.

When we bury rubbish it basically lies rotting and polluting the soil and water sources with toxins and gases for years and years, and this creates 20–40 per cent of greenhouse gas emissions via methane gas. On top of this we are running out of landfill sites, as most are predicted to become full, which means either we start recycling or we start learning to live amidst our trash. Incinerating our rubbish may seem an ideal option but it's not, because burning trash creates CO_2 and toxic gases, which escape into the atmosphere, as well as a huge amount of ash, which then needs to be disposed of in a landfill site!

fact

North Americans throw away 3 kilograms (6½ pounds) of waste per person per day. Every month New Zealanders dispose of enough rubbish and waste to fill a rugby field, and every year on average, each person in the UK throws away seven times their body weight – about 500 kilograms (1,102 pounds) – in rubbish!

What can be recycled?

Thankfully, the recycling possibilities for the things we throw away are huge, with studies showing that 60 per cent of household waste can be recycled – that's paper, glass, some plastics, food, packaging, clothes, shoes, garden waste, tins and even metals. And recycling doesn't just mean ditching the stuff you don't want in a bin for someone else to take away. Recycling includes giving the clothes you don't wear and household items you don't use to charity shops and friends, and also, and just as importantly, thinking about what you buy and why you're buying it, so that you can reduce what you consume overall.

Where to start

Thinking about what you use and why is the best place to start when it comes to reducing your waste, simply because recycling isn't a miracle solution because it also takes energy to do. So if you're guilty of binning shoes because the heels are worn, or throwing out food produce because it's past its sell by date, or even chucking away electrical equipment just because you've been given a spanking-new version, think about what you're doing. If you don't want it, someone else you know might – or someone you don't know – so before you bin it ask yourself:

- Can I reuse this?

- Can I repair this and use it again?

- Can I pass this on to someone who might use it?

- Am I disposing of this in an environmentally friendly way?

- Can this just be dropped in the waste? If it's something electrical, a computer, a mobile phone or batteries you need to dispose of it separately. Contact your local council for details on how to do this.

Recycle this...

Glass

Bottle banks can pretty much be found everywhere these days and are usually divided into separate containers for

holding clear, green and brown glass. All you have to do is remove as many plastic or metal rings and tops as possible. Only recycle bottles and jars – never light bulbs.

Paper

Newspapers, magazines and stationery paper in general are easy to recycle because pretty much every area has a recycling bin for these. Be careful though, not all paper is made the same. Cardboard needs a different recycling pile, and milk and juice cartons cannot be recycled with paper (and in some areas not at all) as they have a plastic lining.

Tin cans

Crush drinks cans before recycling, by squashing them underfoot, although don't try this with tin cans (but do wash them out before putting them in the recycling bin unless you want a maggot attack – and this is usually a requirement if your council is collecting them). You can also put aerosol cans in but they must be empty and obviously should never be crushed.

Clothes

Look for textile banks for leaving your unwanted clothing, which is then sold in charity shops, given to the homeless or sent abroad. Or call a local charity to see if they will collect. Also bear in mind that clothes that are too old

or torn for charity shops can still be put into a textile bank as they are shredded for use as filling for items such as furniture!

Plastic

The problem with plastic is that there are many different types, which means that different reprocessing techniques are required, so always check with your local council to see if (a) they will collect plastic; and (b) if you need to separate or sort your plastics.

Food and garden waste

This is known as organic waste and the best way to deal with it is to compost it, either through a local scheme or at home. Alternatively, you can ask to see if your council supplies food recycling bins and garden waste recycling bags that are collected.

Hazardous waste

For the disposal of hazardous waste such as electrical equipment, batteries, paint, solvents and garden chemicals, contact your local council. Never ever throw them into a normal recycling bin, as they will contaminate the processing, or in the normal waste bin where they will be ditched in a landfill site and potentially contaminate the ground.

Lazy girl recycling facts

- In just one week a newspaper could come back as another paper.
- In just six weeks a metal can could be recycled and used as part of a car or plane!
- In just six weeks plastic bottles can be turned into a fleece jacket.
- Each year, over 100 million mobile phones are thrown away in Europe alone.
- In the US alone, an estimated 12,000,000 barrels of oil are required to produce the 100 billion plastic bags used annually.
- In the UK we throw out 8 billion items of clothing each year.
- Approximately 1 billion trees-worth of paper are thrown away every year in the US.
- Approximately 1.6 million computers are thrown away each year in Australia, most of them into landfill.

Recycling the lazy way

Of course, the laziest way to recycle is to use or find a recycling bin and simply throw your junk in there instead of your normal waste bin. The only problem is that recycling takes energy and power, too, which means it's not always the best eco-choice. Looking at what you're throwing away and why is the first step in being a recycler, because it enables you to reconsider what you're about to discard and whether it has another use or not. This means:

- Reuse something rather than recycling it.

- Buy second-hand rather than new, and we're not just talking clothes but washing machines, household necessities and electrical equipment.

- Pass on books and magazines that you have read to friends and family.

- Reuse plastic bags, ice cream containers and glass jars for storing things.

- Shop wisely by thinking about the packaging you're buying; that is, do you really need four apples in a packet encased in plastic or can you just put four loose apples in your basket?

- Reduce the amount you buy in the first place. For example, how much food do you regularly throw away unused? Or how many items of clothing do you buy and then never wear?

- Avoid buying anything you can't recycle – reuse or refill instead.

- Ask your council about your composting options – some areas will compost your food waste and supply you with green food trash bins or boxes to put your scraps in.

- Separate your recycling into glass, paper, plastics and compost – this saves energy in the long term, as it doesn't need them to be put through a separating process.

The lazy green domestic goddess

Thinking about what chemicals you use to clean your house and reducing the amount you use goes a long way towards being the perfect eco-friendly domestic chick. Apart from ensuring it keeps your air fresher and cleaner, choosing environmentally friendly cleaning products help stop the pollution of the environment (think about how many chemicals go down the plug hole every day, which end up polluting the sewer system and eventually marine life in seas and oceans). Living in a less toxic home is also good news for your health, as being green will help you to sleep better and concentrate more easily as well as reducing your household's effect on the environment. Here's how to do it.

Step 1: Look at what's under your kitchen sink

Bathroom cleaners, toilet bleach, oven cleaners, polishes and even insect repellent are full of chemicals. Remember: if a household cleaner warns you about inhaling the fumes or says, 'danger' or 'caution' on it, it's guaranteed to be full of chemicals, also known as volatile organic compounds (VOCs).

VOCs are dangerous because when inhaled they can cause eye, nose and throat irritation, as well as headaches, loss of coordination and nausea; they can also cause damage to the liver, kidneys and central nervous system.

Step 2: Go natural with your cleaning

To save money, protect your health and reduce energy, use what's in your cupboards alongside green-friendly cleaners to keep your house sparkling fresh and clean.

- **Lemon juice** to remove limescale and bleach your chopping board.

- **Soda crystals** to clean your fridge and work surfaces.

- **Bicarbonate of soda** Mix with water to produce a solution that dissolves dirt and grease. Use to remove stains from the carpet.

- **Malt vinegar and white wine vinegar** Dilute with water to cut through grease and use as a mild disinfectant.

- **Olive oil** Use sparingly as a furniture polish.

- **Tea tree oil** Effective on mould and mildew around the shower and bath.

- **Use old clothes** as dusters and old brushes as scourers.

- **Use plants** to detox your living air – a spider plant near your computer will absorb formaldehyde and benzene; a rubber plant in your kitchen will remove formaldehyde; a peace lily in your bedroom will remove acetone; and a fern in your living area will add humidity to the air. These pollutants get into the air from paints, wood finishes, water heaters, pipes and even your heating system – every house has them, so don't panic.

Step 3: Don't be fooled by the advertising

Five years ago the American Medical Association issued a statement saying that antibacterial soaps were no more effective against germs than ordinary soap. This is because although they may initially kill more bacteria on the skin than regular soap, within an hour or so after use there is no difference in the number of microbes on the skin. Similarly, whereas antibacterial surface cleaners may initially remove more organisms than soap and water, within 90 minutes there is no difference in the number of bacteria that has repopulated cleaned areas.

Step 4: Think about what you're polluting

Think about the products you use to clean up. It's great that you can spray something onto your pans and relieve them of weeks of built-up grease, but if you can't breathe it in – as the warning on the back suggests – should you be washing it down the sink? It's going to flow straight into the sewer system and pollute water that is then discharged into the seas and oceans. Should you even be releasing it into the air you breathe? Read the label – if you have to use gloves to protect your skin, avoid inhaling it and keep it away from delicate surfaces, ask yourself, is it worth using at all?

20 ways to be green at home

1 Change your light bulbs

Only 10 per cent of the input power in a traditional light bulb is converted into light, the rest is lost in heat. Lighting from an LED bulb is more efficient as it can convert 50 per cent of input energy into light. A US Department of Energy report estimated that if LED bulbs were used widely by the population of the US it would have alleviated the need for 133 new power stations in the US.

2 Use a clothes line

Reduce tumble-dryer use with a clothes line. Whether you use an indoor drying rack or an outdoor clothes line, natural drying is better for your garments (look at the lint on your tumble-dryer filter, which fills up with every load – this is your clothing being worn away). Plus, drying your washing on a line is cheaper and doesn't waste energy.

3 Use the cold-water wash

Using the cold-water option on your machine – opting for 30°C (86°F) over 40°C (104°F) and 60°C (140°F) – will save 80–90 per cent of the energy costs from washing. The detergent you use is what really makes the difference in wash results, not the temperature of the water.

4 Take your shoes off

Wiping your shoes as you come in and leaving them at the door will cut levels of lead dust in your home by 60 per cent. This is because almost all of the lead dust inside our homes comes from contaminated outdoor soil.

5 Consider CFL light bulbs

Compact fluorescent light bulbs (CFL) are the funny-looking swirly bulbs. They may cost three times as much as a normal energy-saving bulb *but* they use a quarter less electricity and last for years. Remember to recycle them, though, as they contain 5mg of mercury, so they aren't supposed to end up in a landfill.

6 Reuse containers

Why buy kitchen storage containers when you can reuse old packaging such as large yogurt pots, glass jars and ice cream containers? At the same time, reuse old plastic bags; an estimated 3 billion kilograms (6.6 billion pounds) of plastic bags, wraps and sacks enter the waste stream each year.

7 Don't replace – use it up

You may be tempted to go all out and be green in every aspect of your home life, but before you ditch all your old cleaners, and white electrical goods (fridge, washing machine etc), bear in mind the waste you're creating. It's greener to use up what you have first than replacing everything and throwing goods away, even if they aren't eco-friendly!

8 Avoid leaving the fridge open

Each minute the fridge door is open takes three minutes of energy to then cool the food down again.

9 Use less paper

Every year 900 million trees are cut down to provide materials for paper mills. Help lessen the load by using both sides of the paper you print on, recycling all paper products and thinking about the packaging you buy your products in.

10 Use a microwave to cook

Cooking with a microwave is faster and more efficient than using an oven and will reduce your energy usage by about 75 per cent.

11 Dim your lights

Dimming your lights by 25 or 50 per cent with a dimmer switch saves energy by the same amount.

12 Put your heating on a timer

Unless you live in a freezing climate, no one needs the heat on at night. Set a timer for your heating to switch off at bedtime and back on in the mornings and you could save 25 per cent on heating costs and even more in terms of energy.

13 Don't buy bottled water
Buy a water filter (unless you live in a country that doesn't have good tap water) and simply filter your water instead of buying water that's bottled in plastic bottles.

14 Get a home energy audit
To find out how green your abode is, ask your energy company for a home-energy audit. Most utility providers will do this for free and will tell you how much energy you use and what you can do to reduce it.

15 Recycle all your drink cans
The energy saved by recycling one diet cola can could run a television for three hours!

16 Don't charge your mobile phone overnight
Most phones take only an hour (or less) to charge. If you keep them plugged in all night, all you are doing is drawing electricity for no reason. So unplug the charger and while you're at it switch your phone off. Are you really going to take a call at 3 am?

17 Take your DVD off standby
Eighty-five per cent of energy used by a DVD player is wasted when it's on standby.

18 Use rechargeable batteries
Six-hundred million batteries are used in the UK alone every year – most end up as toxic components of landfill.

19 Reuse plastic bags
Forgetfulness is the reason behind why we use over 500 billion plastic bags every year – or rather a million a minute. It will take over a millennium for these to degrade in a landfill site.

20 Open your windows
Air your house when it's chilly outside (and get rid of some of the those VOCs) and open the windows wide when it's hot. Turn off the air conditioning and/or fans – you'll feel better and save energy.

chapter 2

Beauty, health and fashion

Okay, so you know going green is about recycling and maybe buying organic but, believe it or not, it's also about the clothes you wear, the cosmetics you use and the pills you pop for a headache. Why? Well because everything, even your lipstick, affects the environment. Here's how to be a greener beauty chick.

fact

EU countries have eliminated 450 chemicals from their cosmetics that are known or strongly suspected of being carcinogens or reproductive toxins. In the US only nine have been banned.

Eco-beauty

How much make-up is in your cosmetic bag? And while you're looking, check to see how many toiletries and personal healthcare items are piled up on your bathroom shelves. If you're a low-maintenance kind of girl you're probably thinking that you don't use that much, but consider the shower gels, soaps, shampoos, conditioners, antiperspirants, tampons, toothpaste and cotton wool you get through in a month, never mind a year. Add to that the small luxuries such as bath foams, body creams, nail varnishes and beauty treatments, and you'll see that your carbon footprint when it comes to looking good, although nicely pedicured, is probably fairly large.

The cost of beauty

Studies show the smallest number of products most of us use to beautify ourselves is ten items. That's ten products that get washed down the sink and ten products that come in a variety of packaging and ten products that are thrown away and affect the environment in some way due to the way they have been manufactured, used and/or disposed of.

Of course, at first glance it may seem that something as small as make-up or shower gel has no impact on the outside world, but consider how many of us use these products and how much is then just happily washed down the sink into our sewers and our water systems every day. Environmental studies show that this type of 'beauty' pollution has thrown wildlife into disarray and even affected the way animals reproduce and survive. Think of it this way: if a product can dye your hair from blonde to black, or a cleanser can wash off your foundation, powder and mascara in one go, what's happens to it when it goes down your drains and gets swallowed by marine life?

This is just one reason to think green when it comes to beauty and fashion, but other reasons include your health and your social responsibility. We all assume our beauty products are 100 per cent safe, yet, compared to the amount of testing food and drugs go through, cosmetic production is less stringent and fairly toxin-heavy; meaning, the foaming agents that froth up your shampoo and soap, and the chemicals that create your hand cream are far from natural and organic, and do seep into your skin. Experts say your skin may, on average, absorb up to 60 per cent of 200 chemicals daily.

What's more, think about who's making your products and clothes. Are they kids in a sweatshop or are they people working in a factory with fair wages? Whereas it's tough to think about these things, and then even tougher to give up your favourite brand of lipstick or trainers, using your spending power wisely and buying from companies that advocate fair trade (and other issues you believe in, such as being against animal testing or child labour) is one of the easiest ways to be a lazy eco-girl.

fact

The average woman applies 126 ingredients and chemicals onto her skin daily. Think that sounds a lot of items to use? Well, the majority come from fewer than 15 products: soap, cleanser, toner, face cream, foundation, mascara, lipstick, eye shadow, face powder, shower gel, deodorant, body cream, hair product, shampoo and conditioner.

Where our beauty products go

The main problem is that many of the products we use pass into the skin and are then excreted through our bodies, down the toilet and into the sewers. On top of this, other ingredients – soap, shampoo, conditioner, hair dye, face washes, and so on – get washed down the drain and straight into our rivers and seas. If you consider that the majority of us do this, you can start to imagine why beauty is a green issue. Currently, studies in the US show that some of these washed-away beauty ingredients have been linked to problems with wildlife such as the feminisation of fish (a

problem, because how are they supposed to reproduce if they're all female?) and this is mostly due to the chemicals in our beauty products that mimic our hormones. In fact, according to research from the Environmental Working Group, 50 per cent of beauty products on the market contain an added 'fragrance' made up of a variety of chemicals, which when washed away harm wildlife.

Counting up the waste

Next, think about how much waste there is in the whole beauty business. Aside from the packaging, in a lifetime how many make-up containers, pieces of cotton wool and cans of aerosols/sprays do you think you use and throw away? Think of it this way: if you use just two or three cotton-wool pads a night to take off your make-up, that's approx 90 in a month, and over a 1,000 in a year! If you use two cotton buds a day, that's over 700 in a year! Hair spray, deodorant, shaving foam – maybe you're using as many as four cans a month, that's nearly 50 cans a year!

The lazy girl solution is to buy beauty products that are biodegradable and environmentally friendly. Look for cotton buds that don't have a plastic component or use a face cloth that can be washed instead of using cotton wool. Better still, choose a brand of make-up that either comes in recycled containers or can be recycled by the manufacturer. While you're at it, do away with perfumes and stick to natural fragrances only, buy eco-friendly lipstick and opt for creams, shampoos, bath foam and oils that are organic, fair trade or support local communities and indigenous groups.

Beauty toxins

The problem with our make-up is that we never think twice about what we're using because we assume because it's on sale it's safe. Yet, in recent years one group of chemicals known as phthalates have been linked to health and fertility risks, and are found in a whole list of products, including body lotions, hair spray, perfumes and deodorants, as well as cleansers, nail varnishes and shower gels. Whereas the chemicals have been banned in all European Union as well as Australian and New Zealand products they are still used in the US, Canada and other countries. Having said that, the majority of modern cosmetics and toiletries are complex mixtures of industrially produced, synthetic chemicals. Take nail varnish and nail-polish removers, which are essentially mixtures of toxic chemicals. Many of the solvents and substances used in nail varnishes such as toluene, acetone and formaldehyde have been found to cause health problems in workers, including occupational asthma. Current legislation also does not restrict the quantities or combinations of fragrance chemicals that may be used in cosmetics. According to the cosmetics industry a typical cosmetic often contains between 50 and 100 fragrances.

fact

Ninety-three per cent of British women use cosmetics in some shape or form, making them one of the highest users in Europe.

fact

It has been estimated that as much as 50 per cent of the cost of a bottle of perfume can be accounted for by packaging and advertising.

Lazy girl toxic-beauty checklist

Here's what are in your products:

- **Perfumes** Many contain artificial musks, which don't have to be listed under current health regulations and can affect the immune system.

- **Hairsprays** These can contain benzaldehyde, which, if inhaled, can act like a local anaesthetic and irritate the lungs.

- **Nail-varnish remover** This contains acetone, which depresses the central nervous system and can cause nausea when inhaled.

- **Nail varnish** This can contain camphor, which is absorbed through body tissues leading to twitches and vomiting.

- **Shampoo** Often contains certain phthalates that can enter through the hair follicles and cause hormonal imbalances.

- **Deodorant and antiperspirant** Some have butane and fluorocarbons, which can act like a poison in the body; and many contain parabens, which some studies say are possibly linked to cancer.

- **Hair dyes** These contain the chemicals resorcinol, PPD, ammonia and peroxide. PPD, the most important active ingredient in hair dye, and the colourant resorcinol are potent and can have a very strong allergenic effect on the body.

What can you do?

The solution is firstly to shop wisely. If you're not from an EU country, use brands that have dropped some of these toxins (check the labels). Then think about what's in your cosmetics. Whereas it's important to keep the health risk in perspective, what environmentalists are worried about are the effects of repeated exposure and use, much of which hasn't yet been looked into. In recent years some studies show that there are links between pollutants in our products and the rise of chronic diseases such as asthma and eczema, which is why if you're going to make a green choice about your beauty products it pays to know what to avoid. The following can all cause problems:

- **AHAs** (Alpha-hydroxy acids, or 'fruit acids'; including glycolic acid and lactic acid.) Effects: may increase sensitivity to sunlight, therefore increasing photo-ageing and the risk of sun-related skin cancers.

- **Artificial fragrances** Effects: can exacerbate asthmatic symptoms. May contain chemicals linked to cancer. Damaging to the liver and kidneys, and toxic to the nervous system.

- **Parabens** (Alkyl parahydroxy benzoates, or butyl/methyl/ethyl/ propyl/isobutyl paraben.) Effects: can mimic oestrogen and penetrate the skin.

- **P-Phenylenediamine** (PPD, or para-phenylene-diamine.) Effects: linked to asthma and allergic disease.

- **Sodium lauryl sulphate** Effects: a skin, eye and respiratory-tract irritant and may damage liver, lungs and the immune system.

Go natural

Next, consider changing brands and going natural. Green, and even organic, beauty is a large and expanding market, which means that if you want to buy into green beauty, even your local supermarket has its own collection readily available – what's more, it's cheaper than the big brands. Shop wisely and you can buy earth-friendly cleansers, biodegradable cotton buds and face cloths, make-up with packaging that's been recycled – your list of options is endless with a little bit of shopping effort. All you have to do is learn to read labels, consider what your products are made from and even ask yourself: do I need this? Even better, with green beauty being all the rage, many global companies have even started to reject ingredients such as parabens, petrochemicals and genetically modified additives.

Watch out for misleading labelling

A word of warning: the words 'natural', 'organic' or 'pure' won't necessarily mean your cosmetics and toiletries are safe and environmentally friendly. Like food labelling, cosmetic labelling is a tricky business, meaning you need to look below the surface to see what it is you're really buying. There are no legal definitions for the words 'pure', 'natural' or 'green' on cosmetic labelling, which means a product can proclaim itself green and natural but when looked at closer will contain only small numbers of natural ingredients and still contain plenty of chemicals. This means that in order to ensure your product is green you need to read the small print.

One-hundred per cent natural

If you want natural green products, don't settle for half-natural and look for products with whole plant ingredients such as natural vegetable oils – coconut, sweet almond oil, apricot kernel oil and wheatgerm oil – and botanicals that are derived from organically grown plants such as chamomile, lavender, geranium and mint.

Questions to ask yourself about the product you're buying:

1. What does this really contain?

2. Is the product tested on animals?

3. Is the product recyclable?

4. Will disposing of it harm the environment?

5. Was this made using exploited labour?

6. Do I need it?

7. What makes it natural?

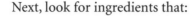

Next, look for ingredients that:

1. Aren't mixed with additives – think essential oils such as rose, tea tree oil and calendula.

2. If you want organic, look for companies that are smaller and use certified organic substances, and/or are leaders in holistic care.

3. Check the shelf life of substances, and then how long they take to biodegrade.

4. Choose containers that display a resin identification code. This code is an international coding system that the American Society of the Plastics Industry Inc. (SPI) introduced in 1988 at the urging of recyclers. The code was developed to meet recyclers' needs and offers a means of identifying the resin content of bottles and containers commonly found in the residential waste stream and working out what can and can't be recycled.

5. Opt for products with minimal packaging and whether you can recycle the whole product after use.

Eco-beauty for free

The good news is that when it comes to getting an environmentally friendly beauty routine, you don't have to spend all your money on expensive eco-creams. The secret is an inside–outside job; meaning, you need to eat well so that your insides can do their magic for the outside. So start by thinking antioxidants. These combat the damage free radicals (pollutants in the air we breathe) do to the skin. Organic fruit and vegetables are the best source of antioxidants because they are easy to buy, low in fat and instant energy boosters.

Beautiful, well-fed skin

Add the following to boost your skin power:

- **To fight the ageing process** Green leafy vegetables (such as broccoli, cabbage and spinach), orange and yellow vegetables (such as carrot and pumpkin) and dark fruit (such as plums, pomegranates and red grapes).

- **To help maintain the structure of the skin** Fruits such as oranges, strawberries, kiwi fruit and nectarines, which are packed with vitamins A, C and E.

Healthy skin also needs an all-round healthy diet to thrive. Aside from antioxidants, eating more fruit and vegetables helps sway you from looking for quick fixes from coffee (which dehydrates the skin), as well as other quick-fix foods that affect your health, particularly chocolate (which causes an insulin high and low) and fast food (which is calorie dense, chemical rich and with no nutrients).

When choosing fruit and vegetables, opt for: a portion of beans or pulses (such as red kidney beans, chickpeas, lentils) a day – these are an excellent source of protein to maintain wrinkle-free skin; pumpkin, strawberries and kiwi fruit – rich in zinc and vitamins A and C, all of which help stimulate blood flow and collagen formation, the skin's support tissue.

Finally, think water – a model's best friend and your beauty ticket to clear, and beautiful skin. Why? Well, for skin to look firm, glowing and young it needs to be hydrated, and the only way to do this is to drink lots of water. And you don't need mineral water (which isn't so eco-friendly), just plain tap water, or filtered water. It's free, it's easy to get hold of and it's the best eco-friendly green beauty choice you can make!

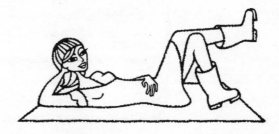

Lazy food on the run

What to eat for healthy eco-friendly skin:

Eat more   Apples
Contains   Selenium and vitamin E
Good for   Antioxidant levels and prevents wrinkles

Eat more   Kiwi fruit
Contains   Copper
Good for   Supplying oxygen to the skin

Eat more   Pumpkin
Contains   Vitamin A
Good for   Maintaining healthy skin and hair

Eat more   Bananas
Contains   Vitamin E
Good for   Minimising the appearance of wrinkles

Eat more   Carrots
Contains   Magnesium
Good for   Detoxifying the skin

Eat more   Berries
Contains   Zinc and vitamin C
Good for   Supporting collagen formation in the skin

Eco-fashion

You may be thinking, how the heck do my clothes affect the climate and environment? Well, for starters, carbon emissions arise in large amounts from the manufacture of clothing. The problem is that the production of textiles is heavily reliant on petrochemical fertilisers and pesticides, which account for a huge percentage of CO_2 and nitrous oxide emissions. On top of this, the demand for man-made fibres has doubled in 15 years, which is bad news again. For example, 65 per cent of the energy consumption from making a T-shirt from a man-made fibre comes from the actual production of the fabric!

Thankfully, being eco-fashionable these days doesn't mean dressing like a hippy and/or wearing only man-made sandals and recycled clothes. In reality it means thinking about what you buy and waste, and considering ethical clothing and/or clothes made from organic sources. It may sound dull, but this means making sure your favourite pair of sexy boots and jeans aren't being stitched together by an impoverished child in a sweatshop in Asia, or that your jeans haven't contributed towards climate change by the way they've been made.

A fair deal

Ethical clothing means that everyone involved in the production of the clothing you buy gets a fair deal in terms of

fact

A T-shirt, if washed at 60°C (140°F), tumble-dried and ironed, will lead to the release of 4 kilograms (8¾ pounds) of CO_2 emissions in its lifetime – the same as a 27-kilometre (17-mile) aeroplane flight.

workers' rights, social justice and environmental issues. In most cases this means the item is made in factories that are inspected so that the people who make your shirt/jeans/ shoes have good working conditions and receive a living wage for their job. In 2004, the EU imported 71 billion euros-worth of clothing. Over 50 per cent of that came from just five countries: China, Turkey, Romania and Bangladesh.

The Fairtrade mark is another international label to look for. This differs from Ethical Trade (which seeks to ensure workers' rights throughout the supply chain of the fashion industry), as it works directly with producers, helping them to access trade, invest in their community development and use sustainable production methods.

Fairtrade certification (usually simply Fairtrade, or Fair Trade Certified™ in the United States) is a product certification system designed to allow consumers to identify products that meet agreed environmental, labour and developmental standards. The FLO (Fair Trade Labelling Organisations) International Fairtrade certification system also covers a growing range of products, including bananas, honey, oranges, cocoa, cotton, dried and fresh fruits, and vegetables, juices, nuts and oil seeds, quinoa, rice, spices, sugar, tea and wine (see Chapter 3 on Green Food).

The good thing about Fairtrade and Fairtrade Certified are that they are independent consumer labels, so this is a 100 per cent guarantee that the people making your clothes are getting a good deal. This is because for a product to display the Fairtrade symbol it must meet the rigorous international Fairtrade standards. This applies all through the supply chain, from the production of cotton through to its manufacture and the printing of the garment.

fact

Cotton uses 22.5 per cent of the world's insecticides and 10 per cent of all pesticides. In America alone, farmers apply 24 million kilos (53 million pounds) of toxic pesticides to cotton fields. Out of the world's total insecticide usage, 25 per cent is used to farm just cotton.

Eco-hostile fabrics

Next, think about what you're wearing in terms of what your clothes are made from. Cotton is the most used fibre in the world, with over 65 per cent of the clothing market using it. So, the next time you pull on a T-shirt, consider that your 100 per cent cotton top is actually only 73 per cent cotton, and the rest is made up of chemicals and resins that were used to grow and make it. And that's the problem with cotton: the production is completely reliant on chemicals that poison the soil, water and even the farmers that work on the land. In fact most textiles have a significant adverse effect on the environment, with at least 20,000 people dying in developing countries each year from poisoning by agricultural pesticides and insecticides. Industrial fibres, in particular, have a negative environmental impact. Polyester, for example, is made from petrochemicals, which means it's not biodegradable, and it involves the intensive use of energy and water in its production. And nylon is reckoned to be responsible for 50 per cent of EU emissions of nitrous oxide – which is another major greenhouse gas!

Go eco-friendly

The solution is to opt for eco-fabrics, or organic or Fairtrade cotton. Organic cotton is defined as: 'fibre that does not come from genetically modified (GM) seed and has been grown without the use of man-made pesticides and fertilisers'. Farming like this means stronger soils and less pollution of water and air. Fairtrade cotton, on the other hand, is cotton that benefits the communities from which it comes. This type of cotton is currently helping more than 95,000 people to improve their lives. However, although organic and Fairtrade cotton clothing is becoming more popular and easier to find, it currently makes up only a tiny percentage of all cotton sales – about 0.1 per cent of global cotton production.

fact

To make the average cotton T-shirt it takes 500 litres (110 gallons) of water and 40 grams (1½ ounces) of pesticides!

Are you a fashion victim?

Finally, consider rethinking your fashion-victim label and looking at how many clothes you buy and use. Between 2001 and 2005 the number of clothes bought per person in the EU increased by over one-third. This is bad news on the green front because most of us have a disposable attitude to clothing; that is, we buy something cheap, wear it once or twice and then throw it away. Of the clothes we decide to then chuck out, 75 per cent ends up in a landfill site, which is why to be green on the fashion front it pays to buy less, think second-hand or vintage when you are out shopping, and give your old clothes to a charity shop.

Vintage/second-hand clothes are ecologically sound because in buying them you are essentially avoiding consuming all the energy used in producing and shipping a new item to your front door; meaning, it's good for the earth and good for your purse. Better still, vintage clothes can be a long-term investment and are easily found everywhere from concessions in high-street stores to eBay, and second-hand clothes stores.

Alongside the above, do your bedroom a favour and de-clutter your wardrobe, handing over unwanted and unused clothes, shoes and bags to charity shops. Recycled clothing currently accounts for 13 per cent of clothes chucked away but could well account for over 80 per cent if we all made it a priority rather than choosing the rubbish

fact

One million tonnes (980 thousand tons) of textiles (mainly clothes from households) are thrown into UK landfills every year, and over 9 million tonnes (8.8 million tons) from US households.

bin! Remember: it might be *your* rubbish but it could be someone else's treasure.

Opt for environmentally friendly fibres

The following are known as eco-fibres and this is due to the renewability of the product; that is, they can be replenished in a relatively short amount of time, and so the size of their carbon footprint (how much land and how few chemicals it takes to bring one of the plants to full growth) is small.

Hemp is by far the crop with the most potential for eco-friendly textile use, as it grows very quickly and is highly pest-resistant. Industrial hemp is harvested for its fibres for hemp clothing and seeds for hemp oil, and has a relatively short growth cycle of 100–120 days. Contrary to popular belief, industrial hemp and marijuana are different breeds of *Cannabis sativa* and smoking hemp flowers will only produce a headache not a high! As for the clothing itself, it's not like sackcloth; in fact hemp clothing is warmer, softer, more absorbent and breathable than clothing made from cotton. It looks like linen, feels like flannel, and wears two to three times longer than other fabrics. Even better is the fact that the majority of the plant can be used.

The seeds are an excellent nutritional source that can provide quality fats and proteins, and the high fibre content of hemp makes it a natural resource for building materials, papermaking, and even biodegradable plastics.

Organic wool Factory-farmed sheep (as with any factory-farmed animals) live miserable lives where the handlers are more concerned with productivity and speed, so the wool isn't so eco-friendly, especially when it's dyed. While factory-farmed sheep are generally kept in the open and not caged in, ewes are made to come into season early by the use of hormones and by being kept indoors with limited daylight which triggers their oestrus. By comparison organic wool comes from sheep which have had no synthetic hormones or been dipped in pesticides to control ticks and lice, and haven't grazed on land with full capacity herds.

Soy silk is made from the by-products of the tofu-making process. The liquefied proteins are turned into fibres which are then spun and used like any other fibre; that is, woven, knitted, and so on. The good things about soy silk, or soy fibres, are that they are a sustainable textile made from renewable natural resources, plus the production is totally harmless to nature. Best of all, soy fibre/soy silk is so soft it's known as 'vegetable cashmere'.

Fortrel EcoSpun™ This is a polyester fibre made out of recycled plastic bottles, which can be made into fleeces. Manufacturing this fibre is preferable to creating new petroleum-based fibres, and super eco-friendly due to the sheer number of plastic bottles in existence.

Organic denim Before they made jeans from cotton, jeans were actually made from hemp, and before that wool! These days most of us, of course, want our jeans to be cotton, but producing jeans is a very non-eco-friendly process. Luckily, there are plenty of companies offering organic cotton, which by comparison typically uses only 350g (12oz) of pesticides and synthetic fertilisers to make one pair of jeans. What's more, natural indigo (rather than synthetic indigo) is used in the dyeing process for organic denim. It is often coloured by a process called 'rope dyeing' during which hundreds of yarns of denim are bundled into the shape of a rope and soaked in a large bath, withdrawn and then oxidised in the air. This process is repeated eight or nine times until the final colour is fixed, and the main advantage is that the waste from the dye has less of an environmental impact.

A word about shoes

Although leather is a completely natural material, the production of it leaves an almighty ecological footprint. This is because the production of it involves solvents, chemicals and dyes as well as huge amounts of water and chromium (VI), which end up polluting water systems. However, while you'll probably always say no to leather trousers, your choices for footwear that are ecologically friendly may not be up your street; that is, plastic and fabric. Thankfully, there are some good alternatives on the market that don't get your feet wet and/or smelly, and if that fails you could always opt for second-hand shoes and/or nix your Imelda Marcos habit!

For lovers of trainers, think about buying a new fashion-able brand called Worn Again (stockists worldwide) made from recycled materials – these shoes are made from 99 per cent recycled materials, such as old T-shirts, leather car seats and army jackets; a percentage from every shoe is given to the company Climate Care who offset carbon emissions.

Green fashion rules

Wear everything you buy – it sounds stupid, but before you go shopping look through your wardrobe and make sure you are wearing everything you own.

Make do and mend

Learn to sew – so that you can mend your clothes. The problem is that whereas our grandmothers would mend all tears and rips, these days it's all too easy to have a disposable mindset about clothes. But the reality is, with maintenance, clothes and shoes can last a long time, so mend rips, sew on buttons, repair the heels on shoes, get rid of stains and don't even think of throwing things away.

Another big leap towards being eco-friendly is to think about how often you wash your clothes. Is a T-shirt you only wore for a few hours really in need of a wash? Do your jeans really need to be tumble-dried? A study in the US found that 60 per cent of the energy associated with a piece of clothing is spent washing and drying it; meaning that over a lifetime, a T-shirt can send up to 4 kilograms (8¾ pounds) of CO_2 into the air. The solution is simple (and, no, it's not to wear dirty clothes), simply wash your clothes when your machine is full, keep the temperature low and hang them up on a clothes line to dry. This way you'll reduce by 90 per cent the CO_2 created by your laundry.

At the same time, don't buy dry-clean-only clothes. The fluid used by more than 85 per cent of drycleaners is nasty stuff called perchloroethylene. This is classified as a probable human cancer-causing chemical by the Environmental Protection Agency, and whereas this chemical poses little health risk to people wearing dry-cleaned clothes, it isn't good for the environment. According to Greenpeace, 70 per cent of the fluid winds up polluting the air or groundwater. Better still, if you avoid dry-clean-only clothes you'll not only help reduce this pollution but you'll save money, too.

Finally, think about your support system: that is, your underwear. What's it made from, what are the ethics of the labour behind it and do you really need 18 bras and 30 pairs of briefs, thongs and magic knickers? The good news is that ethically made eco-friendly underwear is available – what's more it's sexy and comfortable.

Take your bra shopping!

If you want to go to an extreme, Triumph International in Japan recently unveiled a new type of eco-bra that can be converted into a shopping bag. Called the No! Shopping Bag Bra (*NO! reji-bukuro bra*), the environmentally friendly lingerie is designed to promote the reduction of plastic bag consumption (each year Japanese shoppers receive an estimated 30 billion plastic shopping bags, which, in terms of the oil resources needed to produce them, amounts to two giant tankers full of oil). The bra – available in red, blue, green, yellow and pink – is made from the Teijin Group's ECOPET brand of polyester fibre, which has been recycled from plastic bottles through the company's patented EcoCircle recycling system.

Whereas the No! Shopping Bag Bra may be a step too far in the green stakes for you, when thinking about your smalls, remember to think eco-friendly and, if you can't find organic cotton for your undies, consider bamboo – it's sustainable, pesticide free, antibacterial, thermo-regulating and unbelievably soft, so it's actually perfect for knickers, bras and vest tops.

Eco-friendly healthcare

Not many of us ever stop to think what kind of additives, preservatives and toxins are in the medicines, pills and tablets that we take. Whereas you should never completely opt out of traditional medicine or stop taking anything you have been prescribed, for minor conditions think of more environmentally friendly and less toxic options:

Acupuncture

Maintenance of one's energy force (chi), via the placement of very fine needles, has been found to be extremely helpful for fertility problems, period pain and pain management.

Homeopathy

This is based upon the 'like cures like' principle, in that elements that produce certain illnesses can reverse an illness if administered in small amounts. Good for viruses, energy problems and insomnia.

Herbalism

The use of plants and plant extracts to help heal and prevent disease. Good for period problems, and skin disorders.

Osteopathy

This is a form of physical manipulation of the body's joints to help relieve injuries and pain; excellent for sport injuries, back pain and repetitive strain injury.

A word about natural remedies

Although natural remedies provide a range of effective solutions, it should also be noted that just because a product is natural it does not mean that it is safe. Last year alone, millions across the world were spent on alternative products, with one in three people reaching for a natural cure. Whereas no one doubts that plants work (after all, they're the source of many drugs on the market), the problem is that nature packs a powerful and sometimes dangerous punch; meaning that 'ecologically friendly', 'natural' and 'harmless' don't go hand in hand. Part of the problem is that in many countries herbal medicines are not subject to the strict controls, testing and safety regulations applied to all other pharmaceuticals, so whereas they may be natural and good for the environment they may not be so good for you. Also, many of these supplements react with conventional medicine, so don't self-diagnose, and always check with your doctor before taking anything. Lastly, bear in mind that just because a product is natural it doesn't mean that it's organic, or eco-friendly, so read labels carefully.

Keeping natural nice

1. Always see a qualified medical herbalist before taking a natural remedy, if you have a chronic health complaint, are taking prescribed medication from your GP, are pregnant, or breastfeeding.

2. The best place to buy your herbs is from a qualified herbalist's dispensary. If you are buying over the counter, follow the instructions on the label (the label should clearly state both the English and Latin names of the plant, how the plant was grown – that is, whether it is organic – and state a clear dosage).

3. Certain herbs can be used safely at home for small complaints/first aid; for all other problems see a herbalist, who can recommend you see a GP if necessary.

4. If your symptoms do not go away over a reasonable period of time when taking herbs, seek help from a practitioner. Herbal medicine works best when tailored for the individual.

20 *ways* to *be beautifully green, healthy and faishionable*

1 Simplify your life

How many vitamins and supplements do you really need to take? Stop buying them and eat healthily instead. At the same time, look at how many lipsticks/glosses and creams you own. Does your body really need all this – simplify your life, and you'll be amazed at what you save.

2 Less is always more

Again, don't be fooled by the marketing – you don't need perfumed panty liners, a cleanser and toner to wash off your make-up or even heavily perfumed soaps, creams and deodorants (the heavier the fragrance the more chemicals). Go back to basics – you'll save money and stay green.

3 Look for biodegradable formulas

And while you're at it, look for recyclable packaging or at least recycle your waste properly – plastics, glass and aerosols can all be recycled.

4 Opt for lip-gloss over lipstick

That's instead of lipstick, as it contains less potentially toxic colour and fewer film formers to make it stay on for long periods of time.

5 Buy natural, 100 per cent vegetable or organic soaps

Strong soaps are not only harsh on your skin but also have a large environmental impact on rivers and wildlife, thanks to the chemical content.

6 Stop shopping

The greenest garments are those you already own. No more resources are required to get them to you. No more materials' extraction, manufacturing, shipping, retailing, and so on. Oh, and no cost to you.

7 Wash only when you have to
Think full loads in the washing machine only and then air-dry your clothes.

8 Choose greener sanitary products
Seventy-five per cent of all tampons are flushed down the toilet, so try using non-chlorine-bleached sanitary protection, which is more environmentally friendly, or washable menstrual towels, or even menstrual cups (these collect the blood and can be washed out).

9 Go for green toothpaste
In some brands of toothpaste you'll find oestrogen-linked parabens and the detergent sodium lauryl sulphate (SLS), which some countries, such as those in Scandinavia, have discouraged the use of, fearing they may encourage bacterial resistance. Opt for SLS and paraben-free products.

10 Buy a reusable toothbrush
Millions of toothbrushes are thrown away each year, with most people going through an average of four toothbrushes per person per year, and this adds up to 4,389 tonnes (4,320 tons) of waste. With a reusable toothbrush only the head is replaced, and the handle can be reused ad infinitum. This simple waste-saving measure, if used by everyone, would reduce plastic toothbrush waste by 67 per cent.

11 Use half-measures
Less is more. You don't need handfuls of shampoo and conditioner to do the job, or three pads of cotton wool to take off your make-up, or even big dollops of face cream to moisturise your skin. Try to cut down by half the amount you use, by massaging a blob the size of a full teaspoon into your face and skin.

12 Don't be a brand junkie
In other words, shop around. Whereas it's nice to think of yourself as a label beauty queen, experiment with more eco-friendly brands, from cheap to expensive, and see if you can notice the difference.

13 Ditch the all-in-ones

It may seem like an ideal way to waste less, but ready-made facial wipes that do everything take hundreds of years to biodegrade. Instead, invest in a face cloth.

14 Have a clothes/accessories/bag-swap party

De-clutter your wardrobe by getting rid of anything you haven't worn for six months or more (unless it's seasonal) and swap items with friends who are doing the same. It's reusing, recycling and it will save you bundles of cash.

15 Go natural with your medicine cupboard

When it comes to replacing the contents of your medicine cabinet, go natural – try aloe vera for sunburn and burns, tea tree oil as an antiseptic, lavender to aid sleep, peppermint tea for indigestion and arnica cream for bruises and aches.

16 Go green with condoms

If you're a condom user, bear in mind that millions of condoms are put down the toilet across the world each year, and unless you want to see one floating past you in the sea, a landfill is a better place for them than the ocean – so trash them, don't flush them!

17 Be suspicious of hypoallergenic labels

Hypoallergenic, is basically meaningless because even though the main known irritants have been taken out of the product, it will still have other chemicals in the mix that could irritate your skin.

18 Buy an eco-friendly cloth

Eco-cloths stop you using tissues and cotton wool to take off your make-up. It's simply a reusable and washable soft cloth that fits over your hand like a mitten and takes off your make-up when you add water. For pure eco-sense, just cut up old towels and use them as face cloths.

19 **Think about your trainers**
They may not be leather, but most trainers are not eco-friendly, thanks to where they are made, how they are made and the labour used to make them.

20 **Look in your kitchen cupboards for beauty products**
Use oats as a face scrub, olive oil to moisturise your skin and cucumber slices to soothe your eyes. They're cheap, fresh and chemical-free if you use organic!

chapter 3
Green food

Going green with your food is not only good for the environment but also your purse, but if that doesn't convince you, then consider the fact that food is the one area in which it's easiest and most pleasurable to go green and get fantastic environmental results. In fact, the core advice you need can be summed up in just one sentence: buy local produce and you'll help save the world! Why? Well, because local produce is bound to be seasonal and will have a low environmental impact because it hasn't been flown all over the world to get to you (see Green Food Shopping and Food Miles later in this chapter). What's more, locally grown produce is more likely to taste and look like it's supposed to, so you'll have apples that actually taste and look like apples, and tomatoes that are plump and tasty (rather than watery). Plus, the food is less likely to be full of antibiotics, pesticides and chemicals that are pumped in to make produce look perfect, large and durable so that it can survive the long journeys from field to your kitchen table.

Why is now so different?

Of course, you may think: why should I bother to shop, cook and buy differently, as haven't people eaten this way for years and been fine? Well, the truth is that the way we farm, grow and buy food has changed dramatically in the last 20 years. This means that the food that your grandparents and parents ate and drank was considerably different from the food we now buy and digest. This is mainly because food productivity has soared all over the world. Thanks to new technologies, mechanisation and increased chemical use, which all work towards maximising production, we can buy cheaper goods; this is because if food is grown more quickly, it can be sold more cheaply, which means we, the consumers, are happy and will buy more. Although these changes have had positive effects, such as food being cheaper and an amazing choice, the way we eat and shop now has a large impact on the environment.

Apart from driving to the shops and transporting our food all over the world, the way we farm has led to topsoil depletion and groundwater contamination; on top of this, consumer demand has led to more factory farming, more chemicals in our foods and more food scares. This means that if you want to be green in just one way, start by looking at what you are eating and buying.

What to eat (and what not to eat)

The food on our plate adds to the amount of greenhouse gases in the air, simply because mass farming is a major source of emissions such as carbon dioxide, nitrous oxide and methane, all of which are responsible for global warming. However, you can do your bit to save the planet by thinking about the kind of farming that is behind the food you are buying and eating. For example, a recent study found that organic farms use 50 per cent less energy than non-organic farms to produce the same amount of food, which is good news, as less energy use means the release of fewer greenhouse gasses.

So what exactly are you eating? And do you know the difference between GM and non-GM, factory farmed, organic and free range? Or even the reasons why organic is not always the greenest choice? If you don't, here are the answers you need.

fact

Sixty per cent of Americans and Canadians have no idea that they are eating genetically modified foods.

Genetically modified foods

Also known as GM, genetically modified is the scientific term used to describe the insertion of genes into plants and animals. It's done because genetic modification allows them to be produced with specific qualities; for example, vegetables that are resistant to weed killers and pests, or plants that can fruit more abundantly.

The problem with GM technology being introduced into the food chain is the potential risk to human health, including allergic responses to new substances in foods. In reality, GM technology has only undergone a few human feeding trials – and those showed negative results. In one study, commissioned by the UK Food Standards Agency, scientists found that GM DNA is transferring to the human gut bacteria, which is scary, as no one knows what the long-term health implications of this will be. On the environmental front, the other problem is that once GM pollen is released into the environment, there is no way of taking it back, should problems occur. Nor can GM crops be prevented from contaminating other crops. This is why organic food and organic farming prohibits the growing of any GM crops and the use of any GM products, including feed for livestock near their farms.

Wising up to GM

To avoid GM foods, check your food labels, as GM food has to be labelled in all European Union countries, Australia and New Zealand. As yet, the Food and Drug Administration in the US hasn't said that GM food has to be labelled, so if you want to avoid GM in the US, your only bet is to opt for organic. However, it does pay to be aware that wherever you are, certain products don't have to be labelled, such as milk that's come from a cow that has been eating GM feed, so the only 100 per cent guaranteed way to avoid GM is to buy organic.

Factory-farmed food

fact

To fight disease outbreaks and promote unnaturally rapid growth, factory-farmed animals are routinely fed anti-biotics; over 70 per cent of all antibiotics in North America are fed to healthy farm animals.

Factory farms exist to create large amounts of cheap foods, but are essentially inhumane and bad for the environment and your health. It doesn't take a brain surgeon to work out that disease is rife in factory farms, because they crowd tens of thousands of farm animals, such as chickens or pigs, under one roof and provide little or no access to sunlight, fresh air or room for natural movement. Some facilities produce millions of animals each year, so it's little wonder that such large amounts of antibiotics have to be used to keep illness at bay. In the US, almost 50 per cent of all antibiotics are administered to farm animals. These drugs form a toxic residue in animal tissue, but antibiotics are not the only chemicals administered to factory-farmed animals: many animals are fed growth-promoting hormones, appetite stimulants and pesticides, fertilisers and herbicides. In Australia over 13.2 million factory hens produce more than 203 million dozen eggs, each living in a space no bigger than an A4 piece of paper (21 × 30cm/8¼ × 11¾in). The solution: avoid cheap meat and factory-farmed products wherever you can.

Free-range food

Three billion free-range eggs are produced each year in the UK.

Free range usually applies to chickens and the way they are farmed; meaning, they are allowed to move about and eat grubs and are not factory farmed. Free-range chickens, however, are not the same as organic, as they can still be fed antibiotics and additives that add an artificial colour to the egg yolk. Worse still, 'free range' is defined as having eight hours' access to the outdoors each day. In reality less than 15 per cent of poultry in large flocks of 4,000–9,000 birds are able to reach the outdoors (whereas organically reared chickens have a maximum flock size of 2,000, and the use of antibiotics is banned). However, free-range eggs and chicken are better than factory-farmed ones, as tests from free-range flocks have found that, compared to eggs from factory-production systems, the eggs from chickens raised on free-range farms were much more nutritious and up to twice as rich in vitamin E, two to six times richer in beta-carotene (a form of vitamin A) and four times richer in omega-3 essential fatty acids.

Organic food

fact

Due to the lack of pesticides, organic farms have 44 per cent more birds in fields and five times as many wild plants.

Even the laziest of the lazy will have heard of organic food, but do you really know why it's better for you and better for the planet? Well, the number-one reason why organic food is worth considering if you want to be green is because, unlike every other type of food you buy, it has to be produced according to a strict set of principles and eco-standards. These concern the use of pesticides and additives, as well as animal welfare and sustainability; that is, is it good for the earth as well as your stomach?

In normal non-organic food production, around 350 pesticides are permitted and an estimated 4.5 billion litres (1 billion gallons) of them are used annually on foods in the EU, which is why the global organic movement aims for food to be produced in as 'natural' a way as possible that is free from the above and GMOs (genetically modified organisms). At the same time it works on good land management to stop carbon dioxide being released into the atmosphere (soil stores carbon. The more carbon it stores, the less carbon dioxide there is adding to global warming). However, be wary of what you're buying; in EU countries and North America, organic is a regulated term, but in Australia and New Zealand, although exported organic produce must meet the National Standard for Organic and Biodynamic Produce, there is no nationwide regulation to control the labelling of organic food sold within Australia. So if you're buying from an organic retailer, check for the Organic Retailers' and Growers' Association of Australia (ORGAA) notice, which should be prominently displayed, or other organic certifiers such as The National Association for Sustainable Agriculture Australia (NASAA), Organic Food Chain (OFC), Organic Herb Growers of Australia (OHGA), Organic Vignerons Association of Australia (OVAA), and Tasmanian Organic Producers (TOP).

Good food, and animals that are cared for

So here are more reasons why you should buy organic. Firstly, organic meat and produce is free of antibiotics, added hormones and GM technology. In fact animals raised organically are not allowed to be fed antibiotics, or eat genetically modified foods. Animals are also raised in a healthier environment, fed organic feed and often eat a wider range of nutrients than those raised in factory farms.

Secondly, whether you're an animal lover or not, no one

wants to see anything kept in cruel conditions, which is why organically farmed animals are treated more humanely. Factory-farmed animals are kept in tightly confined pens in horrendous conditions. Look for the word 'organic' rather than 'free-range' on meat and eggs, as this means the animals were raised in a more humane way. Their diet also tends to be more well rounded, which means they are given more nutritious food.

Thirdly, with organic food there is far less chemical use all round. This is because organic agriculture works towards a healthy balance of the soil, and uses crop rotation and other techniques to improve soil fertility, instead of controlling the environment with chemicals. The animals are not fed food containing pesticides, and so the amount of persistent pesticides in their fat is reduced. This then safeguards groundwater, topsoil, habitats, and neighbourhood health. Organic farms are therefore more eco-friendly, as they use 70 per cent less energy because they don't use pesticides. The farming techniques of organic farms works on building topsoil so that they don't contribute to soil erosion.

The health benefits

And lastly, organic food is simply better for your health, as it's lower in toxins and more nutritious than conventional food. In one study from the US, organically and conventionally grown apples, potatoes, pears, wheat and sweet

corn were purchased over two years, and analysed for mineral content. The organically grown food averaged 63 per cent higher in calcium, 73 per cent higher in iron, 118 per cent higher in magnesium, 178 per cent higher in molybdenum, 91 per cent higher in phosphorus, 125 per cent higher in potassium and 60 per cent higher in zinc. The organic food averaged 29 per cent lower in mercury than the conventionally raised food. Studies in the UK and Europe have found overwhelming evidence that organic food is more nutritious than conventional food, with the research finding higher levels of vitamin C, higher mineral levels and higher phytonutrients (plant compounds), which can be effective against cancer.

5 lazy reasons why you're not buying organic

1. **The fruit and vegetable looks ugly and odd** That's because you're used to seeing perfect-looking foods on the supermarket shelves. Real food doesn't look anything like the glistening forms found in adverts, but we are accustomed to that *look*, and so naturally inclined to buy things that look healthy and shiny, regardless of whether they actually are. Which is why, long before arriving at your supermarket, non-organic produce will be sorted for

uniform size and shape, whereas organic food is sold in its natural state.

2. **It's dirty** Yes, it's covered in mud because it's fresh and hasn't gone through a lengthy cleaning and packaging process that only prolongs the time it takes from field to table and adds chemicals to the mix. Be realistic: how long does it take to wash an apple, or wash mud off a potato?

3. **It doesn't last long in the fridge** Organic fruit and vegetables go off quicker because fresh and natural food has a limited and natural shelf life. Only food that has been sprayed with preservatives and chemicals has a longer staying power.

4. **It's expensive** Organic food does cost more than non-organic, as production is slower, more labour-intensive and generally has lower yields than conventional methods; meaning, you're paying for the fact that it's better for you and better for the earth! However, if you shop wisely – that is, buy your organic produce direct from a farm or at a farmers' market rather than the supermarket – it's actually cheaper. What's more, if you buy seasonal produce it's cheaper still because it's abundant.

5. **It's hard to find** Untrue; organic produce is everywhere you just have to look for the signs and labels, and ask around.

tip

Beware, having said all of the above, organic isn't always the greenest choice. This is because, as organic food becomes big business, some of its green credentials are misleading. Whereas 66 per cent of the organic primary produce sold in supermarkets is country-sourced in the EU, some organic fruit and salad comes from overseas, making it high in food miles and not so eco-friendly, so check the labels before you buy, and if it's travelled a long distance consider non-organic local seasonal produce instead.

Green food shopping and food miles

When it comes to what you buy, the very first thing you need to think about is food miles. Put simply, food miles are the distance food travels to get from the field to your plate. It's important to consider, because food now accounts for 30 per cent of goods transported on our roads, which means it impacts hugely on the environment by adding massively to the carbon dioxide emissions that contribute towards climate change. On top of this, air transport has the highest CO_2 emissions per tonne (ton) of food and now accounts for 10 per cent of CO_2 emissions from food transport.

Bizarrely and ridiculously, food miles apply whether your strawberries have come from a farm down the road (unless you hand-picked them yourself) or are an exotic brand from abroad, and they are all down to the centralised supermarket systems that insist on packaging foods in certain centres throughout the country before distributing them. A recent German study found that a 240 millilitre (8½ fluid ounce) cup of yogurt on a supermarket shelf in Berlin entails over 9,000 kilometres (5,600 miles) of transportation. (Germans eat 3 billion cups a year.) In the United States, the food for a typical meal has travelled nearly 2,100 kilometres (1,300 miles), but if that meal contains off-season fruits or vegetables the total distance is many times higher.

Food miles affect organic food, too

Even imported organic food can have a tremendous impact. A single Briton's shopping basket of 26 imported organic products could have travelled 241,000 kilometres (150,000 miles) and released as much CO_2 into the atmosphere as an average four-bedroom household does through cooking meals over an eight-month period.

Then there's the other non-organic imported produce. A staggering 1,112,520 tonnes (1,095,000 tons) of vegetables were imported into EU countries last year even when it was possible to grow the products locally. This occurs so that we, the consumer, can have more choice all year round: for example, strawberries when they're out of season. It may sound like good news to you, but this air transportation of food has a greater impact on the environment than sea or road travel. Another reason that produce is imported is labour costs – in many cases it's cheaper to process the food in a different country from that where it was grown and then have it sent back to the original country to be sold. It sounds ridiculous, and it is! To make green choices:

Ask yourself: 'How far has my food travelled?' Although a food's country of origin may be on the label, beyond this it's generally impossible to tell how far the food has travelled and by what means. The means of transport – as well as the distance – is an important consideration. A long journey by boat, for example, has less environmental impact than a shorter one by road. This is part of the reason why good farmers' markets have a policy of selling food from within a defined local area.

Use local shops you can walk to You, the consumer, can make a difference right away by recognising the impact the

way you shop and eat has on the environment. Simply walking to local shops, when possible and buying local ingredients to cook at home has less of an impact than driving to the shops and buying cheaper produce that's been imported.

Buy seasonal local produce Another way to make a difference is to buy seasonal produce from local places. Buying seasonally helps negate the need for artificial heating in glasshouses. It is also important to buy locally grown organic food rather than imported organic food. To give an idea of how far organic food might travel, a typical basket may have travelled the distance of six times around the equator, which means in terms of being green, it isn't!

Use farmers'/local markets These are food markets where local farmers come to sell fresh seasonal produce. Buy your food here and you'll save money, help support sustainable farming, digest less chemicals from your foods and, in turn, help save the planet.

Buy a vegetable box These are schemes whereby you have a seasonal box of organic fruit and vegetables delivered to your door every week or two weeks. You don't get to choose what's in the box, but you're guaranteed that it will be seasonal, organic and abundant.

Pick your own As in straight from the field, rather than straight from the supermarket, all you have to do is look up some local farms and you can pick your own berries, tomatoes, potatoes, corn and even orchard fruit – it's harder work, but it's cheaper and it's eco-friendly.

Grow your own If you don't have a garden, think about finding a local space where you can grow your own. Call your local council for allotment/common land areas (land that you can rent on which to grow produce) or urban gardens you can use. Fruit and vegetables grown on your own land is not only satisfying to eat but is also healthier than pre-packaged goods, as the food retains its goodness (unlike pre-packaged vegetables and salads that have lower amounts of vitamins thanks to the processing procedure). Studies also show that it doesn't take much effort to make things grow, in fact you can grow your own food in a garden with less than an hour's work a day. You'll also be amazed at what you can grow in a window box. As well as herbs such as chives, basil and mint, try tomatoes, salad leaves, rocket and garlic – all eco-friendly, healthy and take zero effort, apart from the odd spot of watering.

Think about the meat you eat

The billions of chickens, turkeys, pigs and cows that are crammed into factory farms each year produce enormous amounts of methane, both in their digestive processes and from the faeces they excrete. Scientists report that every molecule of methane is more than 20 times as effective as CO_2 at trapping heat in our atmosphere. No wonder then that statistics from the Environmental Protection Agency show that animal agriculture is the single largest cause of methane emissions in the US.

So, when buying meat, buy products that come from organic, pastured or grass-fed animals. This is because animals at pasture don't generate the waste-management problems that animals in confinement do. Pastured waste is assimilated back into the soil naturally. In contrast, waste from factory-farmed animals is liquefied and stored, and then sprayed over crop fields, much of it then flows into streams and rivers. If you can't buy pastured meat, buy organic meat. The animals' feed is grown without pesticides, and their waste is not laden with antibiotics and hormones. In factory-farmed animals when the waste washes into the streams and rivers, the feed-additives in the waste then enter the aquatic ecosystem.

Are there plenty more fish in the sea?

Sadly, contrary to the saying, there aren't plenty more fish in the sea. In fact, thanks to our fishing techniques and pollution, stocks of many fishes are now dangerously low, which is why the United Nations Food and Agriculture organisation reported that nearly 70 per cent of the world's fish stocks are overfished or depleted. If you don't want to contribute to the further decline of fish, either don't eat fish or choose your fish carefully. For example, cod stocks are overfished and are among the most heavily depleted. So you should avoid eating cod to help reduce the impact on fish stocks.

Another issue with fish is food miles. Increasingly, fish from the EU are air-freighted into China, where labour costs are lower, and processed there before being flown back to European Union countries, and this happens all over the world.

Globally, fish such as Chilean swordfish and farmed salmon is flown 12,900 kilometres (8,000 miles), and Australian lobster 16,900 kilometres (10,500) miles just to reach Europe, and fish from the North Atlantic is flown to Australia. Finally, there are also a number of issues, both environmental and ecological, associated with farming fish. Take farmed salmon, for example. Chemicals and

treatments used on the salmon can pollute the surrounding waters, so the best choice is to buy organic salmon certified by organic certification bodies. Organic salmon production means that chemical usage is kept to a minimum, sites are carefully selected and fish feed is manufactured from filleting waste from fish used for human consumption.

Water

fact

A huge 2.1 billion litres (500 million gallons) of bottled water was drunk in the UK last year, and 26 billion litres (6 billion gallons) in America, but by far the biggest consumer of bottled water is Italy: about 184 litres (40½ gallons), or more than two glasses of the bottled stuff, is drunk per Italian per day.

Despite bottled water costing around 500 times as much as tap water, we spend endless amounts of money each year on it, which makes zero eco-sense. The best way to reduce the environmental damage caused by using bottled water is to drink tap water wherever possible, recycle all plastic water bottles that you might buy, and even re-use them, or simply buy your water in a bio bottle (see point number

13 in 20 Ways to Green Up Your Food). Why? Well, because 1.5 million barrels of oil in the US alone are used to make water bottles from polyethylene, 86 per cent of which are then dumped in landfills or incinerated. On top of this, bottled water is then transported long distances – which involves burning massive quantities of fossil fuels, all in all making bottled water about the least eco-friendly product you can buy each week.

Say no to packaging

Millions of tonnes (tons) of household waste is generated every year by grocery packaging; think of the bags that wrap your apples and berries, the packaging that comes with ready meals and the shrink-wrapped plastic that's placed over meat, never mind the endless plastic bags your shopping is placed in. Which is why retailers in certain countries have been asked to back a new tax on plastic bags to slash carrier bag use (this has already worked in Ireland), and consider money-back schemes on bottles and the return of excess packaging.

Plastic bags are a huge problem worldwide because they are made from ethylene, a gas that is produced as a by-product of oil, gas and coal production. Generally, there are two types of plastic shopping bags: the lighter, filmy bags you get from supermarkets and other food outlets, and the heavier bags you get from other retail outlets, such as clothing stores. The supermarket bags are made from high-density polyethylene (HDPE), whereas the thicker bags are made from low-density polyethylene (LDPE). Unlike HDPE, LDPE cannot be recycled; which means that if you only want to do one thing to be green – say no to plastic bags and either recycle your bags or buy a cloth one and use that to put your shopping in.

Packaging around the world

See what countries across the world are doing and what can be done to reduce glass, plastic, paper and metal waste:

- **New Zealand** The Packaging Council of New Zealand and the Ministry for the Environment have brought together brand owners, retailers, importers, manufacturers, recyclers and local government, and have established a Glass Forum to keep glass recycling on track and carried out the successful recovery of 72 per cent of paper packaging.

- **In Australia** Kellogg's® use 15,000 tonnes (tons) of cardboard packaging made from recycled paper.

- **In South Africa**, where an estimated eight billion plastic bags are used annually, the government has implemented new regulations that will see only thicker, more durable plastic bags produced, as well as making them more suitable for reuse.

- **In Belgium** stores refund deposits on plastic and glass bottles.

- **In Germany** you can return packaging to the supermarket.

- **In Ireland** by charging €0.15 for every plastic bag, the number of bags used has fallen by a billion a year.

- **In Greece** shoppers are encouraged to buy in bulk, and this cuts down on packaging.

- **In Denmark** packaging is based on natural biodegradable products such as corn starch.

- **In Italy and Spain** when you have finished your wine, you can go to *vino sfuzo/bodega* wholesalers to refill their bottles from vats instead of buying more bottles.

Be aware of additives

Additives are all the artificial sweeteners, colourants and preservatives thrown into our food to make it look brighter, and to keep it long lasting. A list of additives can be found on any food label and is basically any ingredient that sounds scientific and/or you've never seen being sold on a supermarket shelf. The problem with additives is that they are chemical-based and have a direct effect on your body and can make you feel tired, lethargic and bloated, and lead to allergies such as eczema. The good news is that by checking labels carefully you can avoid eating additives.

Problem additives

Here's what to avoid:

- **Aspartame** A well-known sweetener that can cause nausea and headaches – found in diet drinks and foods.

- **Hydrogenated fat** Artificially modified fat that is linked to heart disease – found in crisps.

- **MSG (monosodium glutamate)** Flavour enhancer that can cause headaches and asthma attacks. Found in processed foods and ready-made meals.

- **Phosphoric acid** Used in fizzy drinks and can cause brittle-bone disease.

- **E621, E220 and E211** E numbers that are preservatives and flavour enhancers that can cause an allergic reaction.

- **E104, E133, E110, E124 and E132** These are all artificial colourings and dyes known as Quinoline Yellow, Brilliant Blue, Sunset Yellow, Camoisine, Ponceau and Indigo Carmine. They are banned in some countries, as they have been linked with health problems and can be found in crisps, ready-made foods, sweets and fast food.

How green is your kitchen?

You've gone out of your way to calculate food miles, opted for organic over factory farmed and even walked to the shops instead of taking the car, but if you want to keep your green choices eco-friendly you need also to look at how you cook and store your food. Why? Well, because the more energy we use, the more we personally contribute towards global warming and climate change. Whereas you may not think how you cook your food adds much to the equation, cooking and refrigerating accounts for a third of all the electricity we use in our homes (and in some cases more). So here's how to green up your kitchen.

Your kitchen appliances

Start by buying energy-efficient appliances. This means the next time you need a new refrigerator, dishwasher and washing machine, buy an energy-efficient one (look for the symbol on the tag telling you this) but don't ditch one that works fine just because it's not eco-friendly (as this doesn't make eco-sense). When you do eventually need to shop for an energy-efficient appliance you should look for:

- The estimated annual energy consumption of the model.

- The energy-efficiency rating.

- The range of estimated annual energy consumption, or energy-efficiency ratings, of comparable appliances.

The more energy efficient an appliance is, the less it costs to run, and the lower your energy bills will be. Using less energy is good for the environment, too, as it can reduce air pollution and help conserve natural resources. However, whether you have an energy-efficient fridge or an old fridge, there are still ways to make it more efficient. Firstly, don't fridge surf for food, as your fridge wastes the most energy when you open the door and allow cold air to drop out and warm air to replace it, the thermostat then has to use more electricity to try to cool it back down again. Next, keep your fridge small and full.

An efficient fridge is one that suits your needs, not your designer urgings. So don't buy a trendy fridge that's too big for your needs. And if you live alone and your fridge is rarely ever full, then cheat by filling up a shelf with bottles full of tap water, this will reduce the energy impact of your fridge (as fridges have to work harder when they are empty). Always be sure to cool things down before putting them in the fridge, as the fridge will have to work overtime to cool down anything that's above room temperature. Likewise, uncovered foods release moisture and make the fridge work harder. Finally, make sure your fridge is positioned well. It needs plenty of ventilation at the back to let the warm air escape; and it shouldn't be next to something warm such as a radiator or in direct sunlight.

Green cooking

Your next eco-friendly option is to think about becoming a green cook. Being eco-friendly in the kitchen takes more than buying the right foods and appliances; it is also about how you do your cooking, or rather how energy efficient your techniques are. Food cooks quicker and so uses less energy if you cover pans and woks with a lid. At the same time, make sure your pan covers the coil of your range – this means that when cooking on a gas ring or electric hob, match the pan to the ring size. If the ring is too big for a pan, 40 per cent of the energy escapes. Another good tip is to stop overcooking your vegetables, and 10 minutes before your food is cooked completely turn off the oven or burner and allow the heat in the pot or pan to continue the cooking process for you.

Then think about using your microwave. This is the most energy-efficient way to cook, because microwaves cook faster and at a lower wattage than conventional ovens. Heat up three meals a week in a microwave rather than in a conventional oven. Four minutes in the microwave creates just 22 grams (¾ ounce) of CO_2 as opposed to 385 grams (13 ounces) in an oven.

Finally, save water when you wash up. The good news is that dishwashers are more eco-friendly than hand-washing, but only if you comply with three rules:

1. Only use the machine when it's full.

2. Don't use the drying cycle.

3. Don't run dishes under a tap before placing them in the dishwasher.

This is because a dishwasher uses only half the energy, and one-sixth of the water, used by hand-washing your dirty plates. Better still, the water used in most dishwashers is hot enough to clean the dishes and it will evaporate quickly from plates if you leave the door open after the wash and rinse cycles are complete so you don't need to put it on a drying cycle.

20 ways
to green up your food

1 Go vegetarian twice a week
Eating one or two vegetarian meals a week is a good choice for the environment, as farming animals produces surprisingly large amounts of air and water pollution, and causes 80 per cent of the world's annual deforestation. It also requires large amounts of water, and livestock worldwide consumes half the world's total grain harvest. This is why choosing organic meat and dairy products raised on sustainable farms helps the environment.

2 Compost your food waste
One-quarter of the average binful is made up of organic waste, which means that all vegetables and fruit kitchen trimmings can be composted on a garden compost heap, and the rest via your local council or recycling agency (check to see if they'll supply you with a separate food bin that they collect): that's leftovers, food that's gone off, trimmings and food you don't want. It can include bones, dry foods and cooked foods. Or install a green cone, which reduces food waste to its natural components of water, carbon dioxide and a small residue. The solar-heated garden unit takes all cooked and uncooked food waste, including meat, fish, bones, dairy products, vegetables and fruit.

3 Don't throw your cooking oil down the sink
Whenever small particles of grease are washed down the drain, they solidify and attach to the inside of the pipes. As more and more particles of grease flow down the drain, they gradually accumulate and can form a large mass. This mass eventually clogs the pipes, blocks the wastewater flow and often results in an expensive backup or a public sewer spill. To be eco-friendly, carefully pour used oil into a strong sealable container, such as an old plastic jar with a lid and dispose of it in the trash bin.

4 Say no to packaging for fruit and vegetables

Instead of throwing out food packaging every time you do a shop, buy unpackaged fruit and vegetables by going to the vegetable counter or grocers and choosing to clean them up yourself.

5 Rethink how you buy milk

If you buy milk from the supermarket, it's very likely that it will be in a Tetra-Pak carton or a plastic milk bottle. The Tetra-Pak cartons, because they are made of different materials fused together, are very hard to recycle, and plastic bottles require lots of energy to be recycled. An alternative is to buy your milk in returnable, reusable glass milk bottles from a milkman or local dairy – check in your local area to see what's on offer.

6 Recycle your booze

Be green about your boozing and opt for organic and local wines over imported bottles (food miles apply to drinks as well) and while you're at it, recycle all your cans and bottles!

7 Start a wormery

A wormery is an easy-to-use and efficient system of converting ordinary kitchen waste into top-quality compost and concentrated liquid feed through the natural action of worms. Thirty per cent of household waste is organic and can be recycled, so by using a wormery you reduce the waste dumped in landfill sites, reduce the need for chemical fertilisers and reduce methane emissions from a landfill site.

8 Think twice about ready meals

Ready meals are basically food that ends up being cooked twice, which is a waste of energy. Then think of all the packaging and the cheap ingredients used (meaning they are more likely to come from intensive farms) and you'll see that it's more eco-friendly (and healthier and cheaper) to cook from scratch.

9 Cut back on meat when you're eating out

The Eat Less Meat campaign is calling for a 15 per cent reduction in meat consumption over the next ten to 15 years. Farms are a major source of pollution and tropical forests are cut down to raise beef.

10 Say no to foil

Instead of regular aluminium foil, buy recycled foil to wrap food in. Recycled foil uses a twentieth of the energy needed to produce regular foil.

11 Say no to all packaging

Most food-packaging material uses some petroleum-based plastic. Look for minimally or unpackaged items instead, or purchase brands that use bio-based instead of petroleum-based plastic. Bread, rice, pasta and grains can all be bought at pick-and-mix places and stored in reused bags.

12 Bring a cloth bag to the shops instead of using plastic bags

An estimated 500 billion to 1 trillion plastic bags are consumed worldwide each year. That's 1 million bags used per minute and less than 1 per cent of those are actually recycled.

13 Buy your water in bio bottles

Bio bottles are made from corn but could also be made from potatoes, rice or beetroot. The corn goes through a fermentation and distillation process and is reduced to an acid, which is then moulded into bottles – which means that after use they can be composted.

14 Know your organic labels

100 per cent organic or *USDA* (US Department of Agriculture) *organic* in the USA means all ingredients are organically produced.
Organic means 95 per cent of the ingredients are organically produced.
Made with organic ingredients means 70 per cent organic.
Certified organic means the produce has been certified by a state government agency.

15 Cook at home more often

Reduce global warming and improve air quality by staying home to eat and lowering your car emissions (if you have to drive to eat out)!

16 Buy dolphin-friendly tuna

Tuna has been linked with the killing of dolphins, as they swim alongside tuna and then get caught in the nets. Although new measures have been bought in, around 1,000,000 dolphins are still killed every year.

17 Avoid single portions

Even if you live alone, you don't need to buy single portions of convenience food; they are ecologically unsound as they use up excess packaging.

18 Don't waste food

It sounds obvious but don't waste the food you buy. Use it, cook it, freeze it or share it – don't let it go out of date and then bin it!

19 Buy eco-foods

As in, buy foods that have less of an impact on the environment, such as rice, fruit and vegetables, compared to meat and dairy.

20 Shop by foot not by car

If you can reduce the number of times you go shopping by car, by either walking or getting public transport, you'll help stop the effects of global warming and stop air pollution.

chapter 4
Travel

fact

The average person in the UK drives their car 8,743 kilometres (5,433 miles) per year, takes the bus for 333 kilometres (207 miles) per year and uses the train for 523 kilometres (325 miles) per year. The average American drives 21,979 kilometres (13,657 miles) per year, rarely takes the train and hardly ever takes the bus.

Whether you own a car or not, it doesn't take a genius to work out that driving isn't environmentally friendly. A 1.8-litre car travelling 19,311 kilometres (12,000 miles) per year produces approximately 4.32 tonnes (4.25 tons) of carbon dioxide, which would take six trees approximately 12 months to absorb. With cars contributing to 12 per cent of the European Union's total CO_2 emissions you can see why road transport is the big green baddie.

If you're feeling pretty smug because you don't own a

car, be aware that you may not be as green as you think. For example, how many times do you call a taxi or happily jump into someone else's car for a short-distance journey that you could easily walk? The fact is it's the car culture and our desire to ride rather than walk that is damaging the environment.

Even if you're super-green and take public transport, walk and/or ride your bike everywhere, it's worth bearing in mind that eco-friendly travel and green transport is also about how many times you hop on an aeroplane for a short or long break. Aviation's impact alone is made worse by the fact that aeroplane emissions happen high up where they can do most damage to the atmosphere – which is why the Intergovernmental Panel on Climate Change says that CO_2 emissions from aircraft need to be multiplied by 2.7 to account for their effect on global warming. Alongside how you travel, eco-friendly travelling also means looking at how ethical your holidays are; meaning, when you go abroad, is your time away doing its bit for the local environment or adding to the local damage?

With so much to think about it's tempting to think your best bet is never to travel anywhere and either to stay at home all day (although think of all the energy you'll use in your house doing that) or simply to make a tent out of recycled T-shirts and pitch it on the nearest green spot for two weeks. Luckily, you needn't take such extreme measures, as there is a lazy green way to travel, and this is it.

Eco-friendly driving

Is it possible to be an eco-friendly driver when we know that car emissions are responsible for a large part of global warming and pollution? The answer is, yes, which is good news because, let's face it, having a car does make life easier, so giving up driving probably isn't on your lazy girl agenda. So here's what you need to know to be a lazy green driver.

Quiz: *how green is your car knowledge?*

Tick one answer in each section and then look at the results at the end to see whether you have green driving know-how.

1. **What's the best way to reduce CO_2 emissions (the chief global-warming greenhouse gas) from a car?**

   ☐ a. Buy a car with a catalytic converter (converts gases into less harmful substances).

   ☐ b. Drive less and use more fuel-efficient cars.

   ☐ c. Drive slower.

2. **What type of car is better for the environment?**

☐ a. A manual.

☐ b. An automatic.

☐ c. Neither.

3. Traffic congestion causes noise and air pollution and costs billions a year. What's the best way to cut it?

☐ a. Congestion charges in all major cities.

☐ b. You should car share.

☐ c. Offices should open at different times.

4. Which of the following will help lessen your vehicle's impact on the environment?

☐ a. Drive smoothly.

☐ b. Drive very slowly.

☐ c. Drive a new car.

5. For the average family car the most economical speed to drive at is:

☐ a. 30 mph.

☐ b. 15 mph.

☐ c. 50 mph.

Results

1. A 0, B 10, C 0

Eco-friendly answer: B – whereas converters can eliminate up to 90 per cent of carbon dioxide (CO_2), hydrocarbons (HC), and nitrogen oxides (NOx) emitted from cars, they do not reduce emissions of CO_2. The only way to do this is to use less fuel all round.

2. A 0, B 0, C 10

Eco-friendly answer: C – whereas once automatics burned more fuel, new designs have narrowed the gap, so there's no longer much in it.

3. A 0, B 10, C 0

Eco-friendly answer: B – every day there are 10 million empty seats in cars. If the average car occupancy were to increase by half (to 2.37 persons) it would lead to a one-third fall in traffic.

4. A 10, B 0, C 0

Eco-friendly answer: A – drive smoothly; erratic braking and acceleration increase fuel consumption.

5. A 0, B 0, C 10

Eco-friendly answer: C – 50–60 mph is the most economical speed, 15 or under is the most uneconomical speed. However, obey speed limits otherwise you risk being green and losing your licence.

Total scores

0–10 Energy-Waster
Oops, there's not a hint of green in you.

20–30 Semi-Green
You're semi-green but it's only a short step to being super-green.

40–50 Eco-Chick
Well done, you're super-green!

Cars — the bad guys?

So why are cars such an environment no-no? Well, the simplest reason is that cars run on fossil fuels, such as oil and petrol, which means that thanks to their emissions, they play a major part in climate change and global warming. Yet, despite this obvious fact, most of us rarely think to lower our impact by sharing journeys or avoiding short journeys, which means there are a ridiculous number of cars on the road. For starters, the single-occupant driver still reigns supreme. Nearly 80 per cent of people drive to work alone in the EU (75 per cent in the US), but if two car drivers shared a journey they could reduce their overall pollution by 60 per cent. Plus, 80 per cent of journeys are less than 8 kilometres (5 miles) and 33 per cent are less than 2.5 kilometres (1 mile) – meaning both are easy to do without the car, which in turn would lower emissions and help slow down climate change. On top of this there are other environmental consequences with cars such as:

Noise pollution

Recent studies show that one in eight UK households suffer from noise pollution from traffic, whereas in the US 40 million Americans are exposed to noise levels that cause sleep disruption, the two largest sources of which are airport and vehicle traffic. Problems related to noise include hearing loss, stress, high blood pressure, sleep loss, distraction, loss of work productivity and a general reduction in the quality of life and opportunities for tranquillity. To help cut down on noise pollution if you drive, keep your car in a good state of repair, drive smoothly and keep your windows shut if you're playing music, preferably with the bass turned down.

Waste

In America alone, 10 million cars are scrapped every year, creating approximately seven billion dollars of un-recycled scrap and waste every year. Approximately 800 million tyres are stockpiled in dumps around the country, creating a serious fire hazard and an ongoing environmental hazard. Every tyre on the road loses 450 grams (1 pound) of rubber per year, spewing minute grains of rubber into the atmosphere and back down into the water supply as well as reaching human lungs. Help avoid this by keeping your car in a good state, even if it's an old banger.

Air pollution

In Europe, air pollution is responsible for 310,000 premature deaths each year, thanks to small particles emitted by cars, which are linked to asthma and respiratory diseases. Whereas most people know that cars are major pollutants, it's a myth that old cars pollute more than new cars. Old cars do not necessarily pollute more. New cars that are not properly tuned and maintained also cause pollution. What's more, unleaded petrol, while better for the environment, will still pollute more than necessary if the car is not tuned and maintained.

To help cut down on air pollution from your car: drive less than four times a week, use public transportation, walk, and if you're going to drive:

- Avoid high speeds.

- Buy a vehicle with a high mileage per litre (gallon).

- Don't overfill your tank with petrol.

- Drive alternative vehicles or alternatively fuelled vehicles, such as electric vehicles.

- Keep your car well maintained, especially the emissions-control system.

- Reduce fuel use as often as possible – bear in mind when buying a car that a vehicle's shape and design features can affect its fuel use.

Premature deaths due to air pollution each year

Germany 65,088	Netherlands 13,123
Italy 39,436	Hungary 11,067
France 36,868	Belgium 10,669
UK 32,652	Czech Republic 7,996
Poland 27,934	Austria 4,634
Spain 13,939	

How to reduce your car's environmental impact

The good news is that if you're super-lazy you don't have to trade in your car for a bicycle. Instead, the way you choose to drive can reduce your car's impact on the environment. Here's how to be an eco-friendly driver:

1. **Learn to drive more smoothly** Smoother drivers save on fuel, wear and tear, and end up having to have their car serviced less often.

2. **Learn to read the road ahead,** which in turn will save fuel because you will be using the accelerator and brake less often.

3. **Don't take the car on short journeys** Walk – it's good for the planet and it's good for your bottom.

4. **Switch off your engine when you're stationary for more than two minutes** This saves fuel.

5. **Control your speed** It can cost up to 25 per cent more in fuel to drive at 70 mph compared to 50 mph, and cost equally as much to keep slowing down to under 30 mph and then accelerating. The key is all in the smoothness of your technique, so aim for less sudden acceleration or deceleration.

6. **Ensure you have the correct tyre pressure** Tyres that are under-inflated increase fuel consumption by 1 per cent.

7. **Think about the fuel you're using** A car with efficient fuel consumption is more environmentally friendly than larger cars, because it produces lower emissions.

8. **Consider diesel engines** or alternative fuels such as LPG (liquefied petroleum gas) and CNG (compressed natural gas) – all have lower CO_2 emissions than standard petrol cars.

9. **Get your car serviced,** especially if it's second-hand, as this will improve its performance and limit fuel consumption, as a simple tune-up often improves fuel efficiency by half. If 100,000 of us went out and got a tune up for our cars, we would save 125,984 tonnes (124,000 tons) of CO_2.

10. **Use air conditioning sparingly,** as it significantly increases fuel use.

11. **Drive away immediately when starting from cold** Idling to heat the engine wastes fuel and causes rapid engine wear.

12. **Accessories** such as roof racks, bike carriers and roof boxes significantly reduce fuel efficiency, so remember to remove them when not in use.

13. **If you're stuck in a jam,** switch the engine off if you expect to be there for more than a minute or two. Cutting the engine will save fuel and reduce emissions.

Eco-friendly fuels and cars

Bio-fuels are alternative fuels that are becoming increasingly attractive to use, as they are made from renewable resources and produce less pollution than other fuels. This is because bio-fuels are carbon neutral, which means that they release only as much carbon dioxide when they burn as was used to make the original oil and this is what helps to reduce global warming. What this basically means is that bio-fuels are made from plants, which take CO_2 from the atmosphere during their growth, so when CO_2 is later released during combustion, the net effect is carbon neutral or carbon zero.

The main alternative fuel of the moment is E-85 – 85 per cent bio-ethanol. This is a renewable fuel made from rapeseed, wheat or sugar beet, and 15 per cent petrol.

Another option is LPG (liquefied petroleum gas), which has lower CO_2 emissions than petrol. LPG burns readily in air and has an energy content similar to petrol, plus it offers an immediate reduction of up to 15 per cent in CO_2 emissions compared with the emissions of a petrol-powered car.

LNG (liquefied natural gas) and CNG (compressed natural gas) come from natural gas, which is the cleanest of all the fossil fuels. Composed primarily of methane, this means that when combusted, natural gas releases very small amounts of harmful emissions into the air. In fact, compared to traditional vehicles, cars operating on compressed natural gas have reductions in CO_2 emissions of 25 per cent, and nitrogen oxide emissions can be reduced by 35 to 60 per cent.

For eco-friendly cars, consider driving a 'hybrid' vehicle; these combine a conventional engine with an electric motor and battery and so there are no emissions. The hybrid battery packs are designed to last for the lifetime of the car – somewhere between 241,400 and 322,000 kilometres (150,000 and 200,000 miles) –the batteries can then be fully recycled and the disposal poses no toxic hazards. And, contrary to popular belief, you don't have to plug these cars in. Technology-wise, energy that is usually lost when a car slows down or stops is reclaimed and routed to the hybrid's rechargeable batteries. The process is automatic, so you don't have to do a thing. Hybrid cars top the list of the most fuel-efficient vehicles on the road and in the five years between 2002 and 2007 sales in the US grew twentyfold, but still only represented 1.2 per cent of the 17 million new cars sold in 2006.

Super-green cars

Hybrid cars are super-green because they gain efficiency from:

- **Regenerative braking** The electric motor that drives the hybrid can also slow the car. In this mode, the electric motor acts as a generator and charges the batteries while the car is slowing down.

- **Periodic engine shut-off** When a hybrid car is stopped in traffic, the engine is temporarily shut off. It restarts automatically when put back into gear.

- **Advanced aerodynamics** to reduce drag.

- **Lightweight materials,** which increase the efficiency of hybrid cars.

fact

Cycling just 10 kilometres (6¼ miles) each way to work instead of driving can save 1.3 tonnes (1.27 tons) of greenhouse gas emissions each year.

Get on your bike

The bicycle is the lazy girl's best eco-friend. Even if you're not going to bin your car or nip your taxi habit, buying a bicycle (and riding it on short journeys) will more than do your bit for the environment. For starters, cycling places is faster and more efficient than taking the car. Plus, it offers a non-polluting and quiet means of transport. Cycling also

10 reasons to get on your bike

1. It's cheaper than a car.

2. It will keep you slim, as cycling can burn up to 400 calories an hour.

3. Bike emissions are zero compared to a car.

4. It's easy to park.

5. You can get to places faster, because you can use cycle lanes.

6. There are tax breaks if you're using a bike for commuting.

7. You can use it for recreational use as well as transport.

8. It will tone your thighs.

9. You can go places a car can't go.

10. You can use a variety of routes, not just the road.

provides a low-cost, healthy form of transport that can save door-to-door travel time for short-distance trips up to 5 kilometres (3 miles) long.

A lazy girl's guide to bikes

Before you opt for a sexy and sleek bike, think twice about what you need for your lifestyle.

A hybrid bike

These are good all-round city bikes and are similar to racing bikes and designed for the road. They're nippy, so good if you're planning to use them for your commute, and sturdy enough to carry stuff about.

A sit-up-and-beg bike

Just like your granny used to ride, these bikes are great if you have plenty to carry or want to feel safe in traffic. Not suitable if you want to weave in and out of traffic.

A mountain bike

Tough-terrain bikes that have good brakes and loads of gears can be used for commuting, but are better for country life and steep hills.

A folding bike

Excellent if you need to use public transport as well, but folding bikes are not so good for bumpy roads or if you need to carry equipment.

Public transport

Another green-friendly way to travel is to make full use of public transport. One person using public transport for a year instead of driving to work saves the environment from 4.12 kilograms (9.1 pounds) of hydrocarbons, 28.35

fact

Most countries are way behind countries such as Holland, which build cycle lanes as a matter of course.

fact

Every bus full of passengers removes 40 cars from traffic.

kilograms (62.5 pounds) of carbon monoxide and 2.22 kilograms (4.9 pounds) of nitrogen oxide. Plus, a person who commutes to work by bus rather than driving saves 910 litres (200 gallons) of gasoline per year. Just one reason why buses are a more environmentally friendly form of transport, particularly in relation to the number of car journeys needed to carry the same number of passengers.

Trains are also a green form of transport because they use existing tracks, and therefore use less land than roads, although many still spill out ample amounts of emissions. Trams and light railway have an even lower environmental impact than buses, as they use smaller vehicles and tighter rail tracks than conventional trains, which enables them to be constructed within existing built-up areas.

Quiz: how green is your travel knowledge?

Tick one answer in each section and then look at the results at the end to see whether you have green travel sense.

1. What's the worst option when it comes to flying?

☐ a. A long-haul flight?

☐ b. A short-haul flight?

☐ c. A drive across Europe?

2. On a long-haul flight how much CO_2 emissions will one passenger produce?

□ a. Half a tonne (0.5 ton).

□ b. 5 tonnes (4.9 tons).

□ c. 2 tonnes (1.9 tons).

3. What is slow travel?

□ a. An eco-friendly way of travelling.

□ b. A green term to describe someone who travels on eco-friendly cars and planes.

□ c. Someone who never travels.

4. What is ethical tourism?

□ a. Tourism that benefits the locals.

□ b. Holidays at eco-retreats.

□ c. Tourism where you think green.

Results

1. A 0, B 10, C 0
Eco-friendly answer: B – a short-haul flight, because proportionately more fuel is used in take-off and landing, so it's the worst option of all.

2. A 0, B 0, C 10

Eco-friendly answer: C – 2 tonnes (1.9 tons); that's more than a motorist will produce in a year.

3. A 10, B 0, C 0

Eco-friendly answer: A – slow travel involves swapping fast (but polluting) planes for trains, buses, cargo ships, bicycles – anything but flying.

4. A 10, B 0, C 0

Eco-friendly answer: A – ethical tourism is where you think of your environmental and social impact as a tourist on the country you're visiting.

Total scores

0–10 Energy-Waster
You're a jetsetter who likes to live it up when away – good for your lifestyle but bad fro the environment. Compromise and lessen your impact.

20–30 Semi-Green
You're half way to being a green traveller – keep it up, you're nearly there.

40–50 Eco-Chick
You're an ethical tourist – give yourself a pat on the back.

Plane crazy

Thanks to the arrival of cheap flights, the world is now literally anyone's oyster, sometimes for less than the price of a packet of chewing gum! The trouble is, on the environmental front, flying causes a huge amount of eco-damage. Aside from large amounts of emissions being chucked into the atmosphere, there's noise pollution and even tourist pollution to developing countries to think about.

The obvious way to do your bit for the environment is not to fly anywhere and holiday in your own country, which isn't much of a deal if your own country has about two days of sunshine a year and you're looking to soak up some heat. Another solution is to fly less and only when necessary; meaning, if you're travelling in Europe take your car with friends, not a short flight – better still, take the train. If you plan to go across country in Australia or Africa think of a road trip with friends or the bus or train. And if you really have to fly, think about buying carbon offsets.

Offsetting carbon emissions

Carbon offsetting schemes claim to offset the environmental damage of carbon emissions caused by activities such as driving and flying by investing money in projects that save carbon, such as planting trees or investing in renewable energy projects such as wind farms. Climate Care can help you to calculate the impact of your activities in terms of

CO_2 emissions and provides a mechanism for offsetting these. Payments made via the site are spent on renewable energy, energy-efficiency measures and reforestation. For example, for less than the price of a meal, you can offset 1.3 tonnes (1.27 tons) of CO_2 emissions, equivalent to about 6,400 kilometres (4,000 miles) of car travel.

Critics of these schemes say that offsetting accounts for only a fraction of all emissions produced and that they aren't doing that much for the environment; yet, it's a start for any wannabe eco-traveller.

Be an eco-tourist

fact

According to the World Travel and Tourism Council, there are over 700 million international travellers a year, and this figure is expected to double by 2020.

How you choose to holiday can make a real difference (both for the better and for the worse) to your destinations. On the positive side, it can help protect the natural environment, traditions and culture – and improve the local economy. But on the negative side it can destroy the local environment, boost prices beyond that of the local people and lead to the destruction of wildlife and forests.

Tourism itself generates over 10 per cent of global gross domestic product and employs over 250 million people. It is the main money earner for a third of developing nations and the primary source of foreign exchange earnings for most of the 49 least developed countries – meaning it is big business.

Eco-tourism, on the other hand, is a form of travel that minimises the negative impact of tourism on local communities and environments. It doesn't mean you have to backpack everywhere and stay in hostels or spend your whole holiday planting trees; you just have to make a conscious effort to be aware of the effect that your travels are having on the environment around you.

Think small, think ethically

According to the World Tourism Organisation, eco-tourism is considered the fastest-growing market in the tourism industry, with an annual growth rate of 5 per cent worldwide. This represents 6 per cent of the world gross domestic product and 11.4 per cent of all consumer spending! In terms of tourists, this equals over 715 million international arrivals worldwide, according to the World Tourism Organisation. This is not good news for the planet, as the most popular destinations need to maintain a careful balance between preservation and promotion so that tourism will aid the development of poor communities and help support fragile eco- systems. To do your bit, always think small – as in consider staying in a locally owned hotel or with a local family, or even booking with a local tour operator as opposed to opting for a multinational company that will place you in a hotel that won't benefit the locals.

Book tours and excursions that contribute to the local economy and protect indigenous cultures and wildlife – if you're booking these from your home country, research what you're buying into before booking and whether you will be using a local company or not. Also read up on the countries you plan to visit, and dress and act appropriately – this is a part of ethical tourism. Finally, help the local economy by buying local produce – shop at markets or local grocers and buy local crafts and products. And don't be obsessed with thinking you're being ripped off – consider how much you're arguing over in terms of your own currency.

In many destinations, natural resources such as water, wood and fuel are precious. Local people may not have enough for their own needs, so don't waste it by acting as you would at home. Also try to be eco-friendly where you can, forgo the tour bus or taxi and take public transport, hire a bike or walk where possible.

Finally, don't litter. Think before you throw things away, and reuse bottles, plastic bags and other containers, as developing countries aren't geared up to deal with recycling and waste. Also, litter on beaches can harm wildlife, especially whales and turtles who think plastic items are jellyfish and try to eat them, with dire results.

5 holiday no-nos

1. **Breaking coral** It's so easy to do while diving, but can takes years to recover. The damage caused by a typical brush against coral can take 25 years to re-grow.

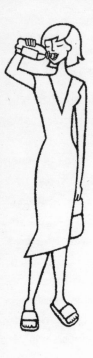

2. **Buying products made from endangered plants or wild animals,** such as hardwoods, corals, shells, ivory and fur.

3. **Throwing plastic bottles in bins** Many developing countries don't have the resources to deal with the huge increase in the number of plastic bottles tourism brings in, especially from bottled water. So avoid buying and bring a reusable bottle with you and fill up from reliable sources as you travel.

4. **Dropping litter on mountainsides,** as you go trekking or mountain climbing.

5. **Wanting to convene with wild animals** The biggest offenders in this category are those who want to swim with wild dolphins or go into shark cages, as these pursuits are said to disturb a marine mammal or the marine mammal stock in the wild by causing disruption of behavioural patterns.

Being a green eco-guest

Even the most ardent eco-person can get a bit sloppy when on holiday, especially when someone else is doing all the clearing up. Suddenly, recycling is something you do only at home, and turning off lights and the TV is something that you 'forget' to do. Here's how to stay green and reduce your waste and energy when you're a hotel guest.

- Say no to having your towels and sheets changed every day.

- Don't use the complimentary bottles of shampoo, shower gel and soap.

- Say no to room service, as it increases waste.

- Avoid long baths and lengthy showers.

- When you leave your hotel room, turn off the air conditioning, heat, lights, TV and radio.

- Take your dirty laundry home.

- Recycle your complimentary newspaper.

- Be sure to turn off sauna, whirlpool, jacuzzi when you're through.

- Check out of the hotel via the hotel's electronic programme available on the TV in some hotels. You can view your bill, approve it and help reduce paperwork.

- Use the hotel van or local transport rather than a hired car.

- Take your waste home instead of ditching half-used toiletries in plastic bottles that you can't be bothered to carry.

- Treat your hotel room the way you'd treat your home; that is, use the same eco-rules you use at home.

20 ways to be a green traveller

1 Be a better driver
Stick to speed limits, drive smoothly, and turn off your air conditioning.

2 Don't be quick to switch cars
A new car may be much greener than a battered old wreck, but keeping your old motor going is greener, as a great deal of energy goes into the manufacture of a car.

3 Think about converting
It may also be possible to convert your existing car to run on other fuels such as LPG.

4 Opt for two wheels
Anything powered on two wheels – even a scooter – will use less fuel than a car.

5 Do your shopping online
It saves you driving to the shops. Or shop locally and walk home.

6 Get on the bus and train
When it comes to greenness you really can't beat public transport. Using the train instead of the plane is an especially sound idea.

7 Share rides more often
The first car-sharing lane on a UK motorway is due to open in 2007 near Leeds, Yorkshire. Look for a local lift-share scheme that allows you to register your journey in an attempt to find a sharer.

8 Remove excess weight
De-clutter your car, as all the junk you've accumulated in it causes the engine to work harder. Whenever the engine needs to work harder, fuel efficiency decreases.

9 Don't idle for long periods of time
Idling for one minute equals the amount of gas used to start the car's engine. If you are forced to sit at an idle, put the car in neutral. Using neutral reduces strain on the transmission and allows it to cool.

10 Don't warm up your car

Older cars required time to let the engine start working. Newer cars are designed to start cold.

11 Don't be a boy racer

Taking off to a fast start burns fuel unnecessarily. This is equal to revving the engine.

12 Open windows in hotels

Fresh air will dilute the concentrated chemical fumes from VOCs – the fumes that come off all the electrical equipment, household cleaners and carpets in hotels – and give you an easier sleep.

13 Take less luggage with you

Unnecessary luggage weight requires 4 per cent of its own weight in fuel every hour during flight.

14 Support local industry wherever you go

This brings income direct to the people who need it – so buy your gifts out of the hotel, eat in local places and use local taxicabs.

15 Eat and buy local food

… as opposed to opting for fast-food chains, and you will kill two environmentally unfriendly birds with one stone; meaning, you'll save on food miles and add income to the local economy.

16 Book through companies who use electronic tickets

Most airlines and some train companies now do this – it's greener and reduces the paper usage.

17 Bring your own toiletries

Many hotels offer soaps, toothpastes, shampoos and more. Using these amenities creates waste from the plastic wrappings, paper boxes and plastic containers they come in. Instead, bring your own toiletries in reusable containers.

18 Ask for glass

If your hotel room comes with plastic cups, ask for a glass. Using this instead of plastic ones will reduce the impact on the environment. Using plastic means throwing away not only the cup but also the plastic wrapper it came in.

19 Don't waste food
If you don't eat all of your

breakfast, consider bagging the rest for lunch.

20 Go green all the way
Fly with an airline that recycles in-flight trash, and use 'green' hotels that offer water-saving techniques and in-room recycling bins.

chapter 5
Lifestyle

What's your leisure time and lifestyle got to do with being ecologically sound? you may ask. Well, just like the food you buy and the way you choose to travel, how you choose to have a good time has an effect on the environment. For example, if you yearn for a plasma screen, or even have one, or listen to digital radio on your TV, or forget to turn your work computer off as you run out the door, or even if you order a latte every day on your way to work, it's worth knowing that these seemingly innocent actions actually cause thousands of extra tonnes (tons) of CO_2 to be released into the atmosphere. For example, plasma screens: if half of all homes were to own one, the UK would have to build at last two new nuclear power stations to meet the electricity demand. Add to this the wasted energy that comes from leaving millions of computers and office lights nationwide switched on all night, or the waste that comes from millions of paper coffee cups and you can see that how you choose to live your life can and does have a major impact on the environment.

So, if you really want to be green or even a bit less lazy about being green you need to stop and think about exactly what you're buying and doing; meaning, putting an end to those shopping binges, consuming less energy when you're relaxing at home, and wasting less all round, both at work and at home.

Eco-friendly home life

You may have changed your light bulbs to energy-saving ones, made your bathroom and kitchen eco-friendly and started cleaning your house the eco-friendly way (see Chapter 1), but when it comes to eco-living there are other home improvements you can make so that your rooms and home become greener. The reality is that our homes account for 27 per cent of all carbon emissions and overall consume three times more energy than driving a car every day to work, so if you want to make a green difference, start by thinking about what you can change around the house.

fact

Fifty per cent of people believe it would cost too much to make their homes eco-friendly.

Step 1: Think about your electrical equipment

This is not just about switching everything off standby (see Chapter 1) but about the sheer volume of electrical equipment you own and how you replace it or update it. If you're a fairly techno person or an Inspector Gadget-type gal, it's likely you have:

- A television or two (or three).

- A DVD player (or two).

- A radio/CD player or two.

- A computer/a laptop.

- A hairdryer/straightening irons.

- An MP3 player/iPod.

- A phone or two.

- A mobile phone (or two).

Now, ask yourself what do you do when you get bored or want the latest item on the market? It's likely you, like most people, don't think twice about throwing your old product out and buying something new. It sounds ridiculous when you think of it, but most of us are guilty of upgrading our mobile phones every year, buying a new gadget every year, and simply doubling up on computer equipment because we feel we need it.

The problem is that waste from discarded mobile phones, computers and TVs is now a fast-growing environmental problem, simply because if you're naughty enough to chuck these products into the normal refuse bin, you're helping make landfills more toxic. For example, an old battery in a mobile phone will contain enough cadmium to contaminate 600,000 litres (132,000 gallons) of water.

In reality, whether you're green or not, you have to dispose of e-waste carefully because it is extremely hazardous. This means it has to be disassembled before it's binned so that the toxic elements inside can be removed. Environmental groups worldwide fear that if electronics like mobile phones and computers reach landfills in huge numbers, they will cause irreparable damage by leaking toxic metals such as lead and mercury into the soil and groundwater and so contaminating whole swathes of the country.

fact

Globally, most mobile users replace their handsets on average every 18 months.

If it's not broke — don't chuck it!

Studies show that 95 per cent of computers that are thrown away work perfectly well and, in Europe alone, an estimated 105 million mobile-phone handsets are discarded every year and fewer than 10 per cent are recycled.

So, if you are going to opt for the latest and flashest of equipment, your first step should be to contact your local council to find out where to take your old stuff or if someone will come and take it away for you. In many cases, however, you'll be throwing out a perfectly good piece of equipment, which means you can recycle it rather than throwing it out. Recycling electrical equipment means giving your phone to a good cause (see Resources, and always take the SIM card out first), giving your computer to someone else who may need it, such as schools or kids who can't afford one, and even passing on your TV and DVD to a needy family (see Resources for more on how to do this). If your equipment is past its best, then look for non-profit groups that help salvage old computers and phones and put the parts to good use in communities and countries that can't afford the latest product on the market.

Finally, consider the fact that over-consumption is a huge part of the environment problem, which means that one of the best and easiest lazy green things you can do is to stop shopping and stick with what you have; meaning, ask yourself: do you really need the newest TV, an updated computer/mobile phone, and the latest gadget that plays games/music or enables you to email on the move? Of course not, so either make do, or invest in an upgrade on the machine/mobile you already have.

Step 2: Think about your interior-design skills

If your idea of interior design is to put a shade over a naked light bulb, you can skip this section because you're probably being more environmentally sound than you think. However, if your greatest passion in life is to decorate your house, paint walls, invest in DIY and buy furniture, then here's what you need to know.

Paint, stains and varnishes can and do have an effect on the air quality inside and outside your home. According to the US Environmental Protection Agency, paints produce about 9 per cent of the volatile organic compound (VOC) emissions from consumer and commercial products. These are carbon compounds that evaporate at room temperature and react in sunlight to help form smog/pollution. VOCs can cause respiratory, skin and eye irritation as well as headaches, nausea and muscle problems. Beyond VOCs, many paints are made with toxic substances and chemicals that come from non-renewable resources or are energy intensive or polluting to produce.

fact

One study found the average EU dustbin contains enough potential energy to power a TV for 5,000 hours, or heat enough water for 3,500 showers.

Paint in an eco-friendly way

To find an eco-friendly paint, read labels and choose brands that are free of formaldehyde, or simply opt for natural paints. These are made mostly of renewable or abundant naturally occurring materials such as citrus oil, lime, clay, linseed oil and chalk. Natural paints do have some disadvantages. They can cost more than latex or oil paints, many paint stores don't sell them, and they take two days or more to dry rather than the one-day latex paints. However, they are great for the environment and your health, and worth the effort if you think about how long you spend at home breathing in the air as you loll about on the sofa!

Step 3: Choose your furniture well

When it comes to furnishing your house, what you choose to plonk your bottom on has a large environmental impact. This is because some mattresses and sofas are made of petroleum-based polyester, nylon and polyurethane (PU) foam that, especially when new, may give off harmful volatile organic compounds (VOCs, see above). On top of this, these items are hard to dispose of, and, when dumped in a landfill, take centuries to biodegrade. So, if you're buying a new piece of furniture, ask for petroleum-free fills (rather than buying a sofa stuffed to the brim with eco-unfriendly substances!).

Of course, it's not always easy to choose your furniture if you're living in rented accommodation or to find eco-friendly furniture, so counterbalance the non-eco-friendly elements of your house with eco-friendly furnishings such as organic cotton bedding, cushions and covers (see Chapter 2 for reasons why organic cotton is better).

At the same time, think about the wood your furniture is made from. Is it sustainable; meaning, is it wood that can be easily replaced and grown? If you can't be sure it has originated from sustainable woodlands, or other recyclable sources, make sure you avoid hardwoods and tropical woods such as mahogany. Bamboo, for example, is one of the world's most prolific and fastest-growing plants and is able to reach maturity in about four years, compared to the typical 25 to 70 years for other tree species. There are over 1,000 documented uses for bamboo, and new innovations are taking place in home furnishings where bamboo is transformed into ply boards that match the properties of conventional wood. Bamboo is also nature's most sustainable resource, as it's grown without pesticides or chemicals, is 100 per cent biodegradable and naturally regenerative.

Better still, ensure all the wood products you buy are certified sustainable by the Forest Stewardship Council (FSC). This is an international not-for-profit organisation founded in 1993 by environmental groups such as Greenpeace, the Sierra Club and World Wildlife Fund. Its mandate is to protect the world's forests through globally recognised principles of responsible forest stewardship. Alongside the type of wood you buy, it's also important to consider the various types of glues and finishes involved in furniture manufacturing, as VOCs originate in certain furnishings.

Eco-friendly living

When you're out having a good time, the last thing you probably want to think about is your impact on the environment, and yet, as you know by now, every little thing you do has an effect. This means that even nipping out for a quick burger or ordering food affects the environment. Think of a takeaway pizza: you may not have used any energy to cook it, but it comes in a large cardboard box that it's likely you will bin without thinking. What's more,

fact

Each day 63.5 kilograms (140 pounds) of waste packaging is produced by the average restaurant/fast-food outlet. When multiplied by the number of stores in the world, the in-house garbage of some chains is equivalent to over 500,000,000 kilograms (1 billion pounds) of waste every year.

how you choose to enjoy your time off also has an effect, with everything from the gym to Christmas adding to your carbon footprint. Here's how to lessen your impact when you're out and about.

Ditch the gym

If you want to be environmentally friendly, then do not go to the gym. This is not an invitation to become a couch potato but a hint to cut your membership fee and use the great outdoors for your workout instead. Why? Well, consider the waste involved. At your average gym there are bikes, treadmills and stair climbers all plugged into the wall, as well as water coolers, air conditioning and MTV – all for your pleasure. On top of this there are showers, and steam rooms and jacuzzis – all wasting energy and water. To be green you're better off saving your cash, going for a run in the park and drinking fresh water from a water fountain

Forget fast-food burgers

Fast-food restaurants may now be using environmentally friendly, processed chlorine-free products to package their food but on the whole they are not environmentally friendly places. Think of all the waste that happens with a simple cheeseburger, chips and milkshake meal. Worst of all, the international meat industry generates roughly 18 per cent of the world's greenhouse gas emissions and much of that comes from the nitrous oxide that's in manure and the release of methane from bovine waste. Methane has a warming effect that is 23 times as great as that of carbon, whereas nitrous oxide is 296 times as great.

Choose your cappuccino wisely

If you're a coffee addict, the chances are you can be found in a trendy coffee bar at least twice a day, probably ordering a grande cappuccino with extra froth and a squirt of vanilla. Apart from wasting your hard-earned money, think of all the waste involved – two takeaway coffees a day adds up to ten cups a week, 40 cups a month and approximately 500 cups a year. If you're always taking trips to the coffee vending machine at work, bear in mind you're doing no better. Vending machines dispense 6 billion cups per year, using 24,000 tonnes (23,620 tons) of polystyrene annually. This is bad news, as polystyrene can take up to 100 years to biodegrade, and certain plastics up to 450 years. A simple green tip is to bring your own coffee mug to work and wash it out at the end of the day!

The other important option is to think about buying Fairtrade coffee, as 20 million farmers in 50 countries rely solely on coffee for their livelihoods. Fairtrade coffee is not just about getting cash back to the growers (non-Fairtrade coffee means farmers get only a minuscule amount of cash for their crop) but also about helping the farmers to help their communities.

fact

One hundred million people in the US and 70 million people in the UK drink coffee every day.

Ask for Fairtrade

The good news is that most of the high-street coffee chains do sell Fairtrade and ethically sourced coffee, all you have to do when you order your grande cappuccino with extra froth is to ask for it!

Have a greener Christmas

Millions of tonnes (tons) of waste is generated at Christmas, thanks to Christmas cards that are trashed after the new year, millions of Christmas trees, which are bought and then thrown out, and the sheer volume of wrapping paper and packaging that ends up in rubbish and trash bins. Thankfully, to have a green Christmas you don't have to become a Scrooge and avoid the whole holiday season; with a few careful green choices you can reduce your waste and your impact.

When shopping, avoid unnecessary packaging or complicated mixed material packaging, which can make recycling difficult. Whereas it's the lazy girl option to get something wrapped in-store, promise to wrap goods yourself so that you can decide how much excess paper to use. And if you're not sure what to buy, why not give money or charity gift vouchers? This way you can save on packaging and/or literally help save someone or something. If you are going to buy presents, opt for gifts that are environmentally friendly or produced in a sustainable way (see Fairtrade, pages 59–60). Also, support a charity and buy presents from charity catalogues.

Above all, think about cutting down on what you buy in excess of your gifts. Present tags can be made from old Christmas cards. Any kind of unusual paper can be used as wrapping paper and any type of gift paper can be recycled. Better still, buy recycled wrapping paper and use string, ribbon or wool for wrapping gifts, rather than tape. While you're at it, make sure you recycle your Christmas cards. A campaign in the UK ensured the recycling of 58 million Christmas cards (the equivalent 1,150 tonnes (1,131 tons)!). In Australia the eco-charity Planet Ark has recycled 550 million greeting cards and has saved more than 100,000 trees over the last 13 years that would have otherwise been used to make paper.

Most of all, think twice about buying a Christmas tree. If you have to go for one, choose a real tree with roots that can be planted in your garden or kept in a pot until next year. Better still, buy an artificial tree but make sure you're going to keep using it, as many can't be recycled. If you haven't gone for a real tree with roots, or have no garden, contact your council to check if it has a scheme for chipping and composting real trees to produce mulch/soil improver.

Eco-friendly lights

If you are going to go the whole hog at Christmas and light up your house, at least choose energy-efficient LED fairy lights and keep them on for less time. This is because larger old-style lights can use as much as 250 watts per 50 bulb strand, so will cost ten times as much as LED bulbs, which use as little as 2 to 4 watts per strand and can last for 20 years.

Curb your shopping bug

Are you a shopaholic with shoes, countless clothes, CDs, books and make-up spilling out of your room? If so, you're not alone, shopping for most lazy girls is number-one on their list of hobbies. If that rings true for you, it's time to put a green spin on things. Firstly, think about what you're buying, whether you need it and what you do when you're bored with it. The aim with anything you buy should be to reduce (as in, do you really need five pairs of jeans?) recycle (as in, this is so last season but maybe someone else would like it), reuse (as in, this might have a use somewhere else in the house) – if you think like that you're automatically being greener.

Next, you need to consider other ways of buying, especially if you drive to the shops every weekend and come back laden with carrier bags and useless items. Firstly, consider shopping locally so that you can walk and so reduce the emissions from your car. Secondly, think about shopping online. This way you can make full use of Internet auction sites, get your clothes cheaper and save yourself the petrol going to and from the shops.

With all your excess spare time, consider other ways to spend your free time. You could of course lie on the sofa and watch TV, or you could get active and do a bit more for the environment. Check out your local library for conservation activities or volunteer groups in your area. Many charities run local wildlife projects or projects that campaign on local environmental issues.

Give up smoking

Try to kick the habit – not just for your health. Did you know it takes 12 years for one cigarette end to bio-degrade? Cigarette butts are not only litter, but they also cause many serious environmental problems. Many land and marine animals die annually from mistakenly eating cigarette butts. Cigarettes tossed out of car windows are often the cause of forest fires.

Plus, the growing, processing and smoking of tobacco have major negative impacts on our local and global environments. The growing of tobacco involves the use of large amounts of fertilisers, herbicides and pesticides. Many of these are toxic and some contain known carcinogens (cancer-causing agents). In developing countries the use of these substances is often unregulated. As well as threatening the health of plantation workers, the chemicals used can often contaminate village water supplies because of run off from the plantations. Deforestation is another problem associated with tobacco growing. Firstly, forests need to be cleared for large-scale tobacco planting. Secondly, pressure on forests also comes from the heavy use of paper associated with the wrapping and packaging of cigarettes. Modern cigarette manufacturing machines use more than 6 kilometres (3¾ miles) of paper per hour.

Don't chew gum

If you must chew gum, dispose of it in an environmentally friendly manner. Chewing gum is not biodegradable and will just stick to the ground until someone is paid to clean it up, and due to its consistency, discarded gum can't be dislodged by normal street cleaning but only by power washing, manual scraping and cryogenics (freezing the gum). So, if you throw your gum in a piece of scrap paper and into the bin, you will not only help keep the environment clean and cut the cost of removing gum from the streets but you'll also avoid endangering bird life and plant life, and help save water, as power/jet-washing streets to get rid of gum uses 1136 litres (250 gallons) of water an hour. You will also save yourself a possible fine. Ireland fines gum litterbugs, as do certain cities in the US, whereas Singapore has banned chewing gum altogether. This rule

fact

GumBusters International does 10 million dollars of business a year cleaning the streets of gum in Europe, the US, Australia and Japan.

was introduced because of the high cost and difficulty in removing littered gum from public premises.

Get involved with green issues

Finally, instead of thinking of all the things you shouldn't be doing, think of all the things you could be doing for the environment (after all, you need something to do now you're not going to shop all the time). Reasons to get involved in green issues are huge and mostly revolve around the idea that if we all sit back and do nothing, in 50 years' time many of the things we take for granted may no longer be available. Take the Amazon rainforest for example, you may think deforestation there has nothing to do with you, but the Amazon rainforestgenerates 20 per cent of the planet's oxygen, and covers 4,380,500 square kilometres (2,722,000 square miles) in nine countries, and carries 15–20 per cent of the earth's life forms. However, deforestation clears 12,070 square kilometres (7,500 square miles) a year – or six soccer/football pitches a minute – which means that in five decades from now they could be no more.

Across the world, according to the World Resources Institute, more than 80 per cent of the earth's natural forests have already been destroyed. Up to 90 per cent of West Africa's coastal rainforests have disappeared since 1900, and Brazil and Indonesia, which contain the world's two largest surviving regions of rainforest, are being

fact

Businesses produce 40 per cent of a country's carbon emissions, compared with 27 per cent for households.

stripped at an alarming rate by logging and land clearing for agriculture, including farming, cattle ranching, soy-bean plantations and palm-oil plantations. Among the obvious consequences of this is the global effect it has. Trees are natural consumers of carbon dioxide, and the destruction of trees not only removes these 'carbon sinks' but also tree burning and decomposition in the rainforests pump into the atmosphere even more carbon dioxide, along with methane, and are now responsible for 18–20 per cent of global greenhouse gas emissions a year.

Be proactive

You can do your bit to get involved with environmental issues such as helping stop destruction of the rainforests by joining forces with an environmental agency like Friends of the Earth or Greenpeace, or on a local grassroots level with an eco-charity near you. Campaigning to stop issues like deforestation isn't just about signing petitions, it's about making others aware of what's going on, looking at your own personal choices and doing something about the green issues that make you seethe, whether it's fair trade, GM crops, global warming and/or endangered species, and doing something about it.

Eco-friendly work life

At home you may be super-green and switch off lights as you exit rooms, recycle your waste and even badger your family and flatmates to do the same, yet research shows that whereas 85 per cent of eco-warriors do their best at home, less than 50 per cent bother to do it at work, simply because it's far easier to sit back and let someone else take responsibility for green work practices than to do it yourself. However, making an effort to work in a green way can mean a considerably lighter ecological footprint and a healthier and more productive place to work.

fact

Workers in major cities of the EU spend an average of 47 hours per year commuting through rush-hour traffic. This adds up to 3.7 billion hours and 105 billion litres (23 billion gallons) of gas wasted in traffic each year.

Simple things make for BIG changes; for example, get rid of the vending machine at work and buy a kettle and a box of biscuits; you'll save energy and possibly lose weight if you opt for a biscuit over a chocolate bar every day. At the same time, get everyone to bring in their own coffee mugs, cutlery and a plate, and save on using polystyrene cups and plastic cutlery and plates. Think about ditching the air con in the summer – you may be screaming, 'NO WAY!', but consider using blinds on windows and a good-quality fan to stop the sun heating up the room like an oven. An air-conditioning unit uses up around 1,440 watts minimum, whereas a floor fan uses only 100 watts and a ceiling fan as little as 15 to 95 watts.

Also, consider ditching the water cooler with its large plastic bottles and all the road miles the delivery guy has to take to get you refills, and use the tap instead. If you're worried about the purity of water, buy a water filter and keep water in the fridge, it's cheaper and more energy efficient than a cooler!

On top of that, think about how you work – if you're at a desk all day how much electricity do you waste, how much paper do you get through and does anyone bother to switch off lights at night? If you're feeling guilty, relax, there are ways to be a green worker and to help save the world at the same time, here's how:

Optimise your computer

Set your computer to energy-saving settings and always shut it down when you leave for the day. Setting your computer on 'sleep' will mean your machine will continue to suck up power until you get in the next day, whereas off means zero energy wasted. At the same time, turn off your screen saver. A screen saver that displays moving images causes your monitor to consume as much electricity as it does in active use. A blank screen saver is only slightly better in that it reduces energy consumption by only a small amount. The best screen saver is also the best energy saver: turn off your monitor when you're not using it. The next best idea is to use your computer's power management feature to shut down the monitor automatically when it is not in use. This will reduce the machine's carbon emissions by 83 per cent.

Opt for an intelligent power strip and green batteries

If you're attached to printers, scanners, iPods, and numerous other products, consider plugging everything into a power strip with an on/off switch. This way the whole desktop setup can be turned off at once so you don't leave certain components running all the time. Also consider using a new smart/intelligent power strip and intelligent plugs. These help stop what's known as idle current being drawn from outlets when electronics aren't in use. Also consider green batteries, which are formulated to provide an economical and reliable power source for low- to medium-drain applications, such as remote controls.

Reduce your paper mountain

Think about printing on both sides when you print out (better still don't print, and read everything online). Also use unwanted mail as scrap paper and recycle all the paper – that includes junk mail, post you have read, printouts and excess office circulars that accumulate on your desk.

Recycle everything else as well

That's recycle all your waste from coffee cups, sandwich wrappings, soda cans, printed matter and newspapers. Also recycle everything from your office post. Ask the person in charge of stationery to order in recycled paper and envelopes, and use biodegradable soaps and recycled paper or cloth towels in the bathroom.

Use a laptop

Believe it or not, it's more eco-friendly to use a laptop over a desktop computer, as they use less energy. Plus, the processors in laptops are designed to run cooler without the need for the big fan most desktops use.

Unplug your phone charger

It sounds obvious, but most of us leave our phones charging for far too long. According to one mobile-phone provider, only 5 per cent of the energy used by phone chargers is used to charge the phone, 95 per cent is wasted by leaving the phone plugged into the socket.

Work from home

Instant messaging, video conferencing, and other work-flow facilities make it easy to work from home and thus cut out unnecessary travelling, emissions and energy wastage (as a bonus, you get to work in your pyjamas). Also, con-sider the possibility of a shorter working week with a day at home, or longer hours in the office to trade for a day off. Of course, this is all up to your boss; what you have to do is prove you'll be more efficient and cheap at home.

Green your commute

If you can't walk, then ease the emissions by getting a bike or a scooter. Better still, take public transport or at least start a lift-share scheme at work, whereby people in the same area can car and petrol share (see Chapter 4 for more on this).

Switch off in more ways than one

Get your boss to use lighting controls at work. Photocells turn lights on and off in response to natural light levels; for example, on at dusk and off at dawn which are times when you might arrive (if you're an early bird) and when people leave. However, this isn't so efficient in winter or if you're in a windowless room. Occupancy sensors activate lights when you enter a room and turn them off after you leave.

Get your office to recycle old equipment

Everything your office throws away can be recycled – from paper to foods, to plastics, old computers, furniture and even printer cartridges. Start a recycling campaign at work and you'll be amazed at what you've all be wasting for no good reason.

Eco-friendly cash

Do you know what happens to your cash behind your back, where it's being invested, who's making money out of it and, more importantly, what it's doing to the environment? Whereas no one is helping themselves to your cash, it's important to know that the money you save or place in a pension or any kind of trust can be invested by the bank you're saving with in pretty much any venture that works against the environment. This is why it's important to find out where your cash will be going before you start saving.

The word to think about is 'ethical' – as in, is your money being invested in activities that have a positive social and ecological impact? With a little bit of research you can invest in savings accounts, retirement funds and mortgages that are ethical. Broadly speaking, ethical companies are ones that don't cause damage to the environment. So they don't cut down forests, invest in weapons, exploit the workforce or produce products that are harmful or dangerous, but not all companies do the same thing.

Be an ethical investor

If you want to be an ethical investor, you need to start by thinking about what issues are important to you when investing. Is it essential that your money isn't invested in GM foods or weapons? Or are you against animal testing or child labour? It's up to you to decide which areas you want to avoid or which ones you want to invest in and what you can live with and what you can't. Next, research your options by asking for ethical accounts at your current bank; many have ethical accounts but don't offer them to you if you don't ask.

Another way to be green with your money is to use your consumer power and shop with your feet, which means that if you don't like the practices of a local shop, or a supermarket chain or fast-food outlet, don't shop there – go somewhere else and let them know why. Many people think this has no impact, and yet it can have a pretty good ripple effect, whereby your decision can affect others who then do the same until you find you have influenced the shop for the better.

Finally, vote for green issues with your fingers by shopping at eco-friendly sites. Anything you want, from nappies to apples, to beds and Internet service providers can be eco-friendly these days, if you shop around. Remember: buying green means more investments in green products, more green shops and more ecological help all round.

20 *ways* to green up your lifestyle

producing, transporting and processing meat, if you switch to vegetarianism you can shrink your carbon footprint by up to almost 1.4 tonnes (1.37 tons) of CO_2 a year.

1 Recycle your thinking
Stop working on autopilot and ask yourself questions before you do anything. For example, when shopping ask yourself, 'Do I really need this?' Before you get in your car and drive, ask yourself, 'Could I walk instead?' And before you throw anything away, 'Do I know anyone else who could benefit from this?'

2 Work out your waste stream
For one whole day bag your waste and then look at every single thing you throw away. How much can be recycled? How much can you avoid using? And how much did you throw away without thinking? Working out your waste stream is the most effective way to reduce it.

3 Become a vegetarian
Given the amount of energy put into

4 Get others in on the act
The biggest impact you can have on the environment (in a good way) is to share your eco-tips with others, especially at work. For example, you could ask your boss to purchase carbon offsets for corporate travel by car and plane. Arrange an office carpool or ask the office manager to get fair-trade coffee for the coffee machine.

5 Take yourself off mailing lists
Nearly one half of all mail is thrown away unopened because it's junk mail and not recycled. Apart from being a pain, this mail accounts for a huge amount of paper waste. To stop the deluge, simply take yourself off mailing lists.

6 Buy a pot plant
A recent study found that placing a pot plant on your desk can lead to a 45

per cent reduction in headaches and 20 per cent reduction in fatigue, all because plants help neutralise toxins and VOCs in the air.

7 Buy rechargeable batteries

Normal batteries contain heavy metals and, when thrown into landfills, can contribute towards soil and water pollution, so if you use battery-operated radios at work or at home, buy a recharger with rechargeable batteries. You can reuse these batteries up to 1,000 times.

8 Start a magazine recycling group

If you're buying around five magazines a month, think of all the paper you're wasting. So, start a magazine group with your friends whereby you all buy one magazine a month and swap them round before throwing them in the recycling bin.

9 Buy your music online

Downloads avoid the waste that comes with a CD (think packaging and all) and is cheaper and enables you to be green about your music.

10 Be the official switcher-off

Angry that no one is taking your green campaign seriously? Well, take charge and be the person who makes sure that all computers, lights and air conditioning units get shut down at the end of the day.

11 Be sure to say no to direct marketing companies

When you subscribe to a magazine, buy something from a catalogue or online store, or donate money, be sure to tick the box that says: 'Please do not pass on my name or address' – so that your address is not be added to any direct marketing companies (in other words, junk-mail providers). Also, call your credit card companies and banks to make sure your address isn't passed on.

12 Clean up your coffee machine

If you make coffee at home or at work, eliminate paper filters by buying a reusable filter (available at natural food stores). White-paper filters pollute water with chlorine and other harmful chemicals, and although unbleached filters are an improvement, over time this is a waste of vast amounts of paper.

13 Change your toilet paper

If every office and home replaced a 180-sheet toilet roll with 100 per cent recycled toilet paper, millions of trees could be saved a year!

14 Sort out your work water problems

Did you know office workers in the US use enough water every day to fill 17,500 Olympic-sized swimming pools? Unfortunately, much of this water comes from leaky taps. A leaky tap that fills a coffee cup in ten minutes will waste an estimated 13,630 litres (3,000 gallons) of water a year.

15 Paper towels or electric dryer at work?

There's no contest. Did you know that electric dryers are twice as energy efficient as paper towels, even towels made from recycled paper? Although the production of the electricity that powers electric dryers generates greenhouse gases, the production of paper towels is twice as energy intensive and creates more greenhouse gases overall. Also, the manufacture of paper towels emits pollutants, including chlorine, and many paper towels are made from virgin wood rather than recycled material.

16 Take up gardening

Pesticides, pollution and habitat destruction are taking a toll on the birds and insects that pollinate about 80 per cent of the world's food supply (or about one out of every three bites of food we eat). To lend a helping hand, plant a pollinator garden. Yellow, blue and purple flowers will help attract bees.

17 Plant a tree

If the thought of recycled toilet paper doesn't do it for you, then plant a tree. The net cooling effect of one healthy tree is equivalent to ten room-sized air conditioners operating 20 hours a day.

18 Be conscious of your stationery use

Some office supplies are better for the environment than others; for example, try to use paperclips rather than adhesive tape, and use crayons or coloured pencils instead of solvent-based markers. Consider refillable pens and mechanical pencils rather than disposable ones.

19 Don't make litter

It's wasteful and means your trash won't get recycled but swept up and poured into a landfill.

20 Pay your bills online

By signing up to pay your bills and do your banking online you're eliminating a massive paper trail (and saving money, as most global banking companies reward those who'll bank online over those who won't). Aside from saving trees, you're also reducing fuel consumption. If every US home viewed and paid their bills online, the switch would cut waste by 1.45 billion tonnes (1.43 billion tons) a year and curb greenhouse gas emissions by 1.9 million tonnes (1.86 million tons) a year.

chapter 6
A–Z of green living

This is the chapter for the laziest girl out there who can't be bothered to work her way through the book every time she wants to find out a greener way to live. In this section you'll find definitions for what eco-terms mean, and how you can do your bit to help (the lazy way, of course).

A is for alternative living

Alternative living is an ecologically conscious way of living, in that its proponents consciously choose to live in as green a way as possible. In some radical cases people choose to downshift, live only off the food they grow, make their own clothes and only use renewable sources of energy. It's not for the faint-hearted (or the lazy) but you can introduce elements of alternative living into your life by becoming more eco-conscious about everything – from where you throw your empty crisp packets to who you buy your electricity from. Better still, you can adopt elements of the eco-life into your own life with relatively little effort, such as recycling all your waste (that is, throwing it into a recycling bin, rather than a normal one), shopping wisely for food (that is, thinking about what you're buying) and generally switching off lights as you exit rooms, to save energy and lower your electricity bills.

B is for biodegradable

Plastic bags, synthetics, plastic bottles, tin cans and computer hardware – these are some of the things that make life easy for us, but these products are not biodegradable, as in they do not break down naturally. This means that when we dispose of them in a garbage pile and/or landfill site, the air, moisture, climate or soil cannot break them down naturally and so they cannot be dissolved within the surrounding land. This means that as they pile up there is an increased threat to the environment.

Biodegradable products on the other hand are products made from nature, and break down safely and relatively quickly, by biological means, so that they can disappear into the environment. These products can be solids biodegrading into the soil or liquids biodegrading into water.

The bad news is that of all the environmental buzzwords, 'biodegradable' has perhaps been the most misused and is perhaps the most difficult to understand. This is because in the past there have been no regulations, so many products have called themselves biodegradable without any real justification. This means you need to use your common sense to detect if something is biodegradable or not, or how long something will take to break down. A leaf, for example, is a perfect example of a biodegradable product, as it takes approximately a year to become part of the forest floor. Plastics, on the other hand, will never biodegrade in anyone's lifetime, and certainly will never break back down into the petroleum from which they were made. So, think twice about what you're using and consider reuse of non-biodegradable products over biodegradable ones.

B is also for bio-fuels

A bio-fuel is any fuel that derives from biomass; meaning, recently living organisms or their metabolic by-products, such as manure from cows. Unlike other fuels such as petroleum and coal, bio-fuels are a renewable energy source (let's face it, cows are never going to run out of manure), and so as green as they come. These fuels also have the advantage of being 'carbon neutral' because although burning them releases carbon into the atmosphere, they aren't damaging like fossil fuels. For this reason they are championed by environmentalists as a way to reduce CO_2 emissions released into the atmosphere. Currently, bio-energy covers only 15 per cent of the world's energy consumption, mostly in developing countries where it is used for direct heating rather than electricity production. There are three categories of bio-fuels: solid, liquid and gas. Of the liquids used as vehicle fuel, the two most common are bio-diesel, made from oil seeds and, as a replacement for petrol, ethanol made from corn, sugar or grain.

C is for carbon footprint

Your carbon footprint is how much carbon is emitted from your lifestyle – that is, your personal impact on the environment in terms of the amount of greenhouse gases. Your footprint is made up of two parts: the direct footprint and the indirect footprint. The direct footprint takes into account how you live and travel, and the indirect footprint the products you use; that is, how much fossil fuel it takes to manufacture them. To reduce your direct footprint, the main things you can do are not fly and start walking instead of using your car. To reduce your indirect footprint, buy biodegradable products and shop locally, buying produce that hasn't travelled thousands of miles to get to you.

C is also for climate change

Climate change refers to the effect human behaviour (that is, how much energy we waste and how many fossil fuels we burn for energy) has had on the global climate due to emissions of greenhouse gases such as carbon dioxide (CO_2) and methane. Some cynical people still think climate change is a myth, and yet, the world over, climate is changing – from melting ice caps in Antarctica to floods across Asia and heatwaves in Europe.

C is also for CO₂ emissions

CO_2, for anyone who failed chemistry, is the symbol for carbon dioxide, and it's often quoted in environmental issues, because CO_2 emissions have become the most common of the greenhouse gases to contribute towards global warming. Major sources of CO_2 emissions include the burning of fossil fuels for energy and transportation, and the destruction of forests.

D is for doing what you can

When it comes to being green, every little bit helps, which means that if you can't buy sustainable wood for your bed, or organic cotton for your sheets, or even if you can't walk to work, you shouldn't become stressed about it, but simply do what you can for the environment. For example, turn your thermostat down, wash your sheets more ecologically, buy energy-saving light bulbs and make sure that when you do buy a new bed the old one goes to a good home and not the landfill site.

D is also for downshifting

This is about using less and buying less; that is, going from being a high-maintenance type of girl to being a girl who can get by on soap and lip-gloss (OK, maybe a bit more than that). Downshifting is also about consuming less by thinking about what you're buying and whether you need it. If you think you can't make a difference, well think again. Just committing to saving 20 per cent of the energy you use can help reduce emissions and slow down climate change.

E is for eco-warrior

If your definition is someone with hairy armpits, unwashed hair and a hemp shirt who lives in a tree – thankfully you're wrong. Today's eco-warrior can be anyone from a businessman to a barista; meaning, it could be you. Whereas the definition is 'an environmental activist', this term applies to anyone who takes direct action to halt, suspend, or otherwise stop an activity that adversely impacts the environment.

E is also for energy saving

Almost half of the emissions that cause climate change come from things we do every day, like turning up the heating to its highest setting because we're chilly, or using the car for a short journey because we're too tired to walk. All these things waste energy and result in large CO_2 emissions, so if you focus on energy saving (see Chapters 1 and 5 for tips on this) you can do your bit to help slow down climate change.

E is also for ethical

This refers to ethical produce or clothing, and it basically means you are buying products that haven't been sewn, or made, by a child/person working long hours in terrible conditions for practically no money. Ethical spending or saving also means knowing that your money has not inadvertently gone towards chopping down the rainforest or polluting the sea, or buying weapons, and so it is doing something good and decent for the environment.

F is for fair trade

The Fairtrade mark is an independent consumer label, which appears on products as a guarantee that disadvantaged producers/farmers in the developing world are getting a better deal. For a product to display this mark it must meet international standards (these standards are set by the international certification body). If passed, it means farmers receive a minimum price that covers the cost of sustainable production and an extra premium that is invested in local social or economic development projects. What this basically means is that any product displaying this mark ensures that the farmer who has produced it will get a fair price for his product and that money will also go back into the area he lives in to help with further development.

F is also for food miles

Put simply, food miles are the measure of the distance a food travels from field to plate. It's an environmental problem because food now accounts for nearly a third of all goods transported across the world by road and by air, and this travel adds substantially to the carbon dioxide emissions that contribute towards climate change. This means, when buying produce, try to buy local and avoid imported. Also, think about how you shop. We now travel further for our shopping and use the car more often to do it.

G is for global warming

Global warming is the steady, and documented, rise in the earth's surface temperature over the last century. Global warming is largely attributable to the increased accumulation of greenhouse gases in the atmosphere trapping heat. Climate change is, in turn, linked to global warming.

G is also for GM food

GM stands for genetically modified foods, which are foods that have been artificially changed by scientists in a laboratory so that they can be pest-resistant or grow larger, or, in the case of GM tomatoes, be redder. Environmental campaigners are against GM foods because research shows that they could damage our health. Scientists, however, argue that GM technology is the future for food. They say that plants can be bred to fight off weeds and pests, so crops are never spoiled. To avoid GM foods, look at labels before you buy.

G is also for greenhouse gases

These are the gases that trap the sun's heat in the atmosphere, leading to a rise in global temperatures that then cause unpredictable climate change, such as rising sea levels, flooding and droughts. The gases caused by a variety of human behaviour such as the burning of fossil fuels, air travel and car use are carbon dioxide, nitrous oxide and methane.

H is for housework

Eco-friendly housework goes a long way towards doing your bit for the environment, because buying eco-friendly cleaning products (or making your own – see Chapter 1) not only ensures less pollution going down the drain and into the sewer but also a home with clean air. What's more, it will help you to live in a less toxic environment, which in turn will improve sleep and concentration.

J is for junk mail

The environmental impact of junk mail is substantial. More than 100 million trees worth of junk mail arrives in American mailboxes each year – that's the equivalent of deforesting the entire Rocky Mountain National Park every four months! Plus, over 100,000 acres of trees are cut just for catalogues, and pulp processing to produce paper for junk mail requires 114 billion litres (25 billion gallons) of water. What's worse is that over half of all junk mail goes directly into the bin and isn't recycled, making it a mammoth environmental issue. If you won't take steps to stop it piling up on your doorstep, then at least throw it in the recycling bin.

K is for Kyoto

Kyoto Protocol is an international agreement based on stopping climate change reached in Kyoto in 1997. The Protocol established specific targets and timetables for reductions in greenhouse gas emissions to be achieved by all signatories. Eighty-four other countries have now signed the Protocol, but because many countries, including the US, have yet to ratify it, nothing is as yet being done.

L is for litter

Litter, as well as being nasty to see, is also a broader environmental issue. Apart from being harmful to the environment, as most of it isn't biodegradable, it can also hurt and hinder wildlife and pollute the water system. For example, plastic bottles, fast-food containers, cans and cigarette butts make up 70–80 per cent of EU street litter, and cigarette butts alone take up to 12 years to break down.

M is for mobile phones

Mobile phones, aside from being a lazy girl's best friend, are huge environmental wasters unless you use them more effectively. This means recycling your old mobile/cell phones (see Chapter 5) but also thinking when you re-charge them. Ninety-five per cent of the energy used by mobile-phone chargers is wasted energy. Only 5 per cent is actually used to charge phones and the rest is used when the charger is plugged into the wall but not switched off at the socket. That's over 50,000 tonnes (49,000tons) of car-bon dioxide emissions that could be avoided if we all just unplug our chargers after use – the equivalent of almost 500 football/soccer pitches worth of forest every year!

N is for nappies

You may not have a baby right now, but one day you might, which is why it's worth considering the environ-mental impact of nappies. At least 95 per cent of parents use disposable nappies and nearly 90 per cent of these nap-pies end up in landfill sites. Whereas it would be foolish to suggest to the lazy girl that she go down the washable

nappy path, there are ways to lessen your baby's impact on the environment. Either opt for nappies that use fewer or no super-absorbents (usually a plastic layer that won't decompose in a landfill) or try reusables: a basic fabric nappy that is used with a disposable inner section that can be thrown away, as it is biodegradable.

O is for organic

Organic foods are grown without the use of fertilisers and pesticides and all animals are reared without the use of antibiotics. Choosing organic, however, means more than limiting your toxin intake and helping keep soil nutrient friendly. Organic means higher levels of vitamins and minerals and no controversial additives, such as aspartame and hydrogenated fats, and no GM ingredients. This means that if you choose to do only one thing for the environment and your health you can't go wrong with buying organic.

P is for parabens

Parabens are the most commonly used preservatives in cosmetic, personal care and toiletry products. In the past, studies have linked them to a number of illnesses, because parabens are said to mimic the female hormone oestrogen. However, studies are small and not proven. If you're concerned, look for products that are organic or natural, and read the label to be sure they are paraben-free.

P is also for pollution

Pollution means any contamination of air, soil, water and the environment. Air pollution usually comes from the fumes (carbon monoxide, nitrogen dioxide and sulphur dioxide) released from burning fuel, so industry and transport are major sources and you can limit your impact on it by not driving and by thinking about what you buy. Water pollution is all the dirty water and fluids from our houses and factories that we throw down the pipes, which then flow into rivers and oceans. Help stop water pollution by thinking about what you flush away or pour down the sink.

P is also for precycle

Unlike recycling, precycling is something you do before you shop, and the key with it is to think ahead; meaning, work out how you're going to dispose of a product and its packaging before you buy it, and make your purchase choice based on that! To precycle effectively, buy in bulk and look for products that can be used over and over. Bring your own cloth grocery bags to the store instead of accepting paper or plastic, and look for containers that can be used or recycled, aluminium and glass, or ones that can be composted, such as paper.

R is for recycling

Recycling is not just about throwing your newspapers and empty wine bottles into a recycling bin, it's about looking at your waste and seeing how much of it really needs to go into a normal bin and how much could be put to better use. The reality is that nearly everything can be recycled or reused – all you have to do is slim your bin by making an effort. Why? Well, put simply, recycling is brilliant for the environment: it saves energy, reduces the size of landfills and puts your waste to better use.

R is also for renewable energy

As fossil fuels run out, everyone's looking for a better source of energy that quickly replenishes itself and can be used again and again, and this is where renewable energy comes in. These are alternative sources of energy such as wind power and solar power, and even hydroelectric power can be used to generate electricity and power, and heat our homes on an infinite basis.

Wind power is the world's fastest-growing energy source and works by harnessing wind via turbines to provide electricity.

Solar power works by converting sunlight directly into electricity (even on cloudy days) using semiconductor technology. A simpler way is to design buildings to make maximum use of the sun.

Hydro power has been used to provide electricity for over 100 years and presently provides over 1 per cent of electricity.

Geothermal energy comes from hot rocks deep underground. In some parts of the world steam comes to the surface and can be used to run steam turbines to produce electricity directly. In other places water can be pumped down and heated by the rocks to make steam.

R is also for reusing

As in, think before you throw something away. Reusing is the sister of recycling because it's all about thinking about whether you can reuse something by getting it repaired, reuse something as something else (such as using an old T-shirt as a duster) or reuse it by giving it to someone else. Better still, if you're looking to make some money, consider if you could reuse the item by selling it on an online site. And remember: reusing covers everything from magazines to paper, clothes, electrical equipment and furniture!

S is for seasonal foods

Buy seasonal and you're not only buying local but also buying produce that's cheaper and has probably travelled less miles and so had less of an impact on the environment. If you're stuck for what's in season, take a walk round the shops and see what fruit and vegetables are in abundance and are going cheap. A lazy girl clue being that if you live in

a cold climate you won't get strawberries and tropical fruit in December unless they are imported. If you can't live without your tropical smoothie, then buy frozen or, better still, pick your berries in the summer and freeze them for the winter months.

T is for toxins

Toxins are agents capable of causing our bodies harm. External toxins come from external sources; for example, car fumes, tobacco smoke, drugs, dental fillings, factory pollution, lead, and so on. This means that to reduce the toxins in your body you need to think about everything from your lifestyle choices to the way you live your life. If you want to reduce your toxin levels, consider the following:

- Giving up smoking.

- Walking instead of driving.

- Eating fast food only once a week.

- Going organic.

- Saying no to processed or packaged food.

- Using only organic and natural make-up.

V is for VOCs

VOCs are volatile organic compounds and are known irritants. Indoor sources include solvents, floor adhesives, paint, furnishings and cleaning products. The problem with VOCs is the associated health effects, which include headaches, dizziness, asthma and skin irritations. To help reduce the pollution inside your home:

- Opt for products with low VOCs (see Chapter 5).

- Make sure you provide plenty of fresh air when using these products.

- Throw away unused or little-used containers safely; buy in quantities that you will use soon.

W is for waste

Waste or rubbish is what we throw away, and if you think about it, almost everything we do in life creates waste, whether it's eating, shopping, partying or even going to work. The problem with waste is that we are now throwing away things in such huge quantities that we are putting pressure on the environment's ability to cope: landfill sites are running out, as are the fossil fuels we need to make new things to replace the things we've thrown away. The answer, therefore, is simple: we all need to cut our waste by buying and throwing away less.

W is also for water

We all waste water, whether it's standing under the shower for ten minutes a day or letting the tap run when we clean our teeth. To help conserve water and do your bit for the environment it's simple, see Chapter 1, but if you can't face doing more than two things:

Don't use the toilet as a wastebasket Every time you flush cotton wool, facial tissue or other small pieces of trash, 23–32 litres (5–7 gallons) of water is wasted; and three-quarters of water wastage happens in the bathroom.

Take shorter showers Another way to cut down on water use is to turn off the shower while soaping up, and then turn it back on to rinse. A four-minute shower uses approximately 91–102 litres (20–40 gallons) of water.

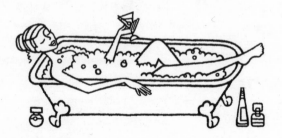

resources

UK

Measuring your carbon footprint

Carbon footprint Work out how big your carbon footprint is and what to do about it: www.carbonfootprint.com
Zero Carbon Footprint How to limit your carbon footprint: www.zerocarbonfootprint.co.uk

Information on the environment

DEFRA (Department for Environment Food and Rural Affairs): www.defra.gov.uk
Earthwatch: www.earthwatch.org
Environmental Protection Agency: www.epa.gov
Friends of the Earth: www.foe.co.uk
Greenpeace: www.greenpeace.org
Global Action Plan: www.globalactionplan.org.uk
WWF (World Wildlife Fund for Nature): www.wwf.org.uk
Women's Environmental Network: www.wen.org.uk

Recycling

For an email list of where you can give away household goods
and furniture you no longer want/need in your local area,
with the aim of keeping things out of landfill sites:
www.freecycle.org and www.uk.freecycle.org
Recycling Guide: www.recycling-guide.org.uk
Recycle More: www.recycle-more.co.uk
Waste Online: www.wasteonline.org.uk
Waste Watch: www.wastewatch.org.uk

Energy saving

Energy Saving Trust: www.est.org.uk
Energy Watch: www.energywatch.org.uk
National Energy Foundation: www.energysaving.co.uk
Green Electricity: www.greenelectricity.org

Water-saving equipment

Hippo the Water Saver: www.hippo-the-watersaver.co.uk
Aqualogic: www.aqualogic-wc.com

Eco-shopping

For light bulbs and household energy-saving products:
Energy Saving World: www.energysavingworld.co.uk
Energy Savers Direct: www.energysavers-direct.com

Ecotopia for E-cloths: www.ecotopia.co.uk
Nigel's Eco Store: www.theinsightecostore.com

Green cleaning products

Ecover UK: www.ecover.com
Ecozone: www.ecozone.co.uk
Green People: www.greenpeople.co.uk
Green Brands: www.greenbrands.co.uk
Love Eco: www.love-eco.co.uk
Simple Green: www.simplegreen.co.uk

Beauty

Barefoot Botanicals Eco-friendly Toiletries: www.barefoot-
    botanicals.com
Burts Bees All products made naturally with recycled
    packaging: www.burtsbees.com
Ecosoapia Eco-friendly Soap: www.ecosoapia.com
Jason's Natural Personal Care Paraben-free factor-30
    sunscreen: www.jason-natural.com
Make Your Own Cosmetics Buy ingredients to make your
    own make-up: www.makeyourcosmetics.com
Mooncup Green sanitary protection: www.mooncup.co.uk
Natural Collection For reusable toothbrushes and
    biodegradable cotton buds: www.naturalcollection.co.uk
The Organic Pharmacy: www.theorganicpharmacy.com

Healthcare

Aromatherapy Consortium: www.aromatherapy-regulation.org.uk

British Homeopathic Association: www.trusthomeopathy.org

Dr Greenfingers Plant-based all-natural first-aid products: www.drgreenfingers.co.uk

National Institute of Medical Herbalists: www.nimh.org.uk

Napiers Holistic treatment using natural remedies and therapies. Also organic skincare, plant and herb remedies available online: www.napiers.net/

Nelsons Homeopathic Pharmacy: www.nelsonspharmacy.com

Osteopathy: www.osteopathy.org

Traditional Chinese Medicine: www.rehm.co.uk

Clothing

Ethical, organic cotton and Fairtrade certified clothes:

American Apparel: www.americanapparel.net

Clean Up Fashion: www.cleanupfashion.co.uk

Edun Ethical clothing: www.edun.ie

Green Knickers: www.greenknickers.org

Howies: www.howies.co.uk

Hug: www.hug.co.uk

Labour Behind the Label: www.labourbehindthelabel.org

The Natural Collection: www.naturalcollection.com

People Tree: www.peopletree.co.uk

Clothing Directory For a list of companies that supply fairly
   traded and/or organic clothing: www.resurgence.org

Spirit of Nature Organic clothing and skincare:
   www.spiritofnature.co.uk

**Traid (Textile Recycling Aid and International
   Development)** Donate old clothes: www.traid.org.uk

Shoes and trainers

Green Shoes Ethically made shoes: www.greenshoes.co.uk

The Natural Shoe Store Vegan and ethically made shoes:
   www.thenaturalshoestore.com

Worn Again For designer trainers: www.wornagain.co.uk

Composting and allotments

Allotments UK Allotments around the UK: www.allotments-
   uk.com

Green Cone For disposing of food waste: www.greencone.com

Green Gardener Eco-friendly garden equipment:
   www.greengardener.co.uk

Wiggly Wigglers How to compost all your organic waste:
   www.wigglywigglers.co.uk

Food

A Lot of Organics Search engine for organic and Fairtrade
food: www.alotoforganics.co.uk

Belu Water in a plastic biodegradable bottle: www.belu.org

Fish Online Sustainable fish: www.fishonline.org

The Fairtrade Foundation: www.fairtrade.org.uk

Local Harvest To find farms, markets and other food sources
in your area: www.localharvest.org

Pick Your Own Farms Add country of origin after web
address to find local farms: www.pickyourown.org

Soil Association For organic news and information:
www.soilassociation.org

Sustain For better food and farming: www.sustainweb.org

Why Organic? Organic food: www.whyorganic.org

Travel and transport

Ecotravel Aims to raise awareness of lower-emission vehicles,
alternative fuels and local air quality:
www.ecotravel.org.uk/fuels

Environmental Transport Association: www.eta.co.uk

Freewheelers Online service for people offering or looking for
lifts in the UK: www.freewheelers.co.uk

Liftshare Find lift-shares in your area: www.liftshare.org

My Lifts Car-sharing website: www.mylifts.com

Tourism

Climate Care The carbon calculator that will allow you to compare travelling by train to flying and will give you your total in tonnes (tons) of CO_2: www.climatecare.org

Coral Reef Alliance Information on viable tourism: www.coralreefalliance.org

Green Globe Sustainable tourism: www.greenglobe.org

The International Ecotourism Society Ecological tourism: www.ecotourism.org

Organic Holidays Organic places to stay around the world: www.organicholidays.com

Tourism Concern: www.tourismconcern.org.uk

Travel Foundation: www.thetravelfoundation.org.uk

Alternative fuels

BioDiesel Filling Stations: www.biodieselfillingstations.co.uk

Bio-Power: www.bio-power.co.uk

LPG Autogas: www.boostlpg.co.uk

Carbon offsetting schemes

Carbon Planet: www.carbonplanet.com

Carbon Trust: www.carbontrust.co.uk

CO_2 Balance: www.co2balance.com

Lifestyle and work

The Carbon Trust Offers free advice to companies looking to save energy at work: www.thecarbontrust.co.uk

Doctor Energy UK power strips/intelligent power strips: www.doctorenergy.co.uk

Domia A wonderous gadget that stops electrical equipment using energy when it's on standby. Plug into a socket and then plug devices into that and it will switch appliances off automatically: www.domia.eu

Earth Share Environmental tips for employers and employees: www.earthshare.org

Eco-Chick Information on how to be green: www.eco-chick.com

Eco-Friend Information on how to lead a green life both at home and at work: www.ecofriend.org

ECOutlet Products for a greener lifestyle: www.ecoutlet.co.uk

Eco-work Sustainable and recycled office furniture: www.ecowork.com

Environmental News Network: www.enn.com

Green Stationery Company Recycled paper and green office products: www.greenstat.co.uk

Recycled Products A directory of products and stationery made from recycled materials; contains over 1,000 products: www.recycledproducts.org.uk

Woodland Trust Where to recycle Christmas cards and trees: www.woodland-trust.org.uk

Mobile phones

The Recycling Appeal: This appeal has generated over £2 million for partner organisations since 1999, including Breast Cancer Care, Oxfam, National Childbirth Trust and the RNIB (Royal National Institute for the Blind) to name but a few. It works by you sending your old mobiles, PDAs and printer cartridges to your chosen appeal. The Recycling Appeal then uses approved recycling partners to recover the products that can be reused or recycled: www.recyclingappeal.com

Action Aid For recycling mobile phones, PDAs and ink cartridges: www.actionaidrecycling.org.uk

Fonebak Specialises in recycling mobile phones: www.fonebak.com

Junk mail and calls

Direct Marketing Association: www.controlyourpost.co.uk
Mail Preference Service To stop junk mail by post:
    www.mpsonline.org.uk
Telephone Preference Service Register to make sure your
    telephone number is no longer available to telephone
    marketers: www.tpsonline.org.uk

Home furnishings and DIY

The Alternative Flooring Company: www.alternative-flooring.co.uk

Arbor Vetum Environmentally friendly furniture: www.arborvetum.co.uk

Eco Organic Paints: www.ecosorganicpaints.com

Eco Paints: www.ecopaints.eu

Eco Home Store: www.ecohomestore.co.uk

Forest Stewardship Council For FSC-certified wood: www.fsc.org

Furniture Reuse Network To recycle your old furniture: www.crn.org.uk

Green Fibres Organic bedding, mattresses and beds: www.greenfibres.com

The Healthy House Organic bedding and eco-friendly cleaners and paints: www.healthy-house.co.uk

Organic Towel Company: www.organictowel.co.uk

Money

Ecology Building Society: www.ecology.co.uk

The Ethical Investment Co-operative: www.ethicalmoney.org

Ethical Investment Research Services: www.eiris.org

Investing Ethically: www.investing-ethically.co.uk

Profit with Principle: www.profitwithprinciple.co.uk

Australia and New Zealand

Australian Mobile Telecommunications Association (AMTA)
Mobile phone recycling: www.amta.org.au

Buy Organic For all things organic, including bamboo
underwear: www.buyorganic.com.au

Carbon Neutral Carbon offsetting company:
www.carbonneutral.com.au

Friends of the Earth International: www.foei.org

Greenpeace Australia: www.greenpeace.org/australia

National Water Commission: www.nwc.gov.au

Energy Labeling: www.nwc.gov.au

Energy Save: www.energy.com.au

Foods Standards: www.foodstandards.gov.au

Organics Australia Online For eco-friendly products:
www.organicsaustraliaonline.com.au

Organic Federation of Australia: www.ofa.org.au

Organic Food Directory: www.organicfooddirectory.com.au

Organic Food Delivery: www.fresh2u.co.nz

Organics New Zealand: www.organicsnewzealand.org.nz

Pick Your Own Farms Add country of origin after web
address to find local farms: www.pickyourown.org

Planet Ark Environmental news: www.planetark.com

Recycling Australia: www.recyclingaustralia.com

Recycling Near You: www.recyclingnearyou.com.au

Reduce Your Rubbish: www.reducerubbish.govt.nz

Zero Waste New Zealand Trust: www.zerowaste.co.nz

Canada

Canadian Recycling: www.recycle.nrcan.gc.ca

Canadian Organic Growers: www.cog.ca

Friends of the Earth: www.foecanada.org

Happy Hippie Directory of eco-friendly goods: www.happyhippie.com

Health Goods: www.healthgoods.com

Planet Friendly: www.planetfriendly.net

Sage Creek Organic cotton clothing: www.sagecreekcanada.com

Transport Canada For news of environmentally friendly bus and road services: www.transport-canada.org

Tree Canada Carbon offsetting: www.treecanada.ca

USA

Aubrey Organics Certified organic skin care: www.aubrey-organics.com

Carbon Fund Carbon offsetting: www.carbonfund.org

Carbon Neutral Shop Eco-gadgets: www.carbonneutral.com

Computer Recycling USA: www.computerrecyclingusa.com

Diva Cup Green sanitary protection: www.divacup.com

Eco Action: www.eco-action.net

Energy Saving: www.energyguide.com

Envirolink Non-governmental organisation supplying online environmental resources: www.envirolink.org

Friends of the Earth International: www.foei.org

Global Green Hybrid Cars: www.globalgreen.org

Green Pages Directory of American Green Businesses:
www.coopamerica.org

I Love Mountains Helping stop the destruction of mountain-
tops for coal mining: www.ilovemountains.org

Loomstate A new US denim label that uses 19th-century,
pre-industrialised farming and manufacturing methods
to weave raw organic cotton yarn: www.loomstate.org

Mail Preference Service To get off of national mailing lists,
send your name, address and signature to: Mail Preference
Service, c/o Direct Marketing Association, P.O. Box 643,
Carmel, NY 10512

Natural food Hub Directory of natural foods:
www.naturalhub.com

National Recycling Coalition: www.nrc-recycle.org

Smart Home USA Smart strip power US and Canada:
www.smarthomeusa.com

Undo Global Warming Information on global warming:
www.undoit.org

Zero Waste Information on recycling:
www.zerowasteamerica.org

Index